The Unmasked: The Untold Journey of Damian Charles Caynes, The Troll Killer

The Troll Killer, Volume 1

Dr. Charlize Deenan Greyson

Published by FutureVision Publishing, 2024.

The Unmasked: The Untold Journey Of Damian Charles Caynes, Troll Killer

Written By

Dr. Charlize Deenan Greyson

Dedicated to "The Most Tenacious D of the 21st Century", The Troll Killer Himself, Dr. Damian Charles Caynes.

"The Unmasked: The Untold Journey of Damian Charles Caynes, The Troll Killer" is a captivating non-fiction book that delves into the remarkable life and extraordinary achievements of Damian Charles Caynes. Fueled by a deep sense of justice and a relentless determination to combat online abuse, Caynes emerges as an unassuming hero in the world of internet trolls.

Introduction

"The Unmasked: The Untold Journey of Damian Charles Caynes, The Troll Killer" is a captivating non-fiction book that delves into the remarkable life and extraordinary achievements of Damian Charles Caynes. Fueled by a deep sense of justice and a relentless determination to combat online abuse, Caynes emerges as an unassuming hero in the world of internet trolls.

In this intriguing narrative, readers are taken on a rollercoaster ride through Caynes's tumultuous personal journey. From his humble beginnings as a regular internet user to his transformation into a formidable troll hunter, the book explores the defining moments and experiences that shaped Caynes's unique perspective and unwavering commitment to fighting online harassment.

Through vivid storytelling and intimate interviews with those close to Damian Charles Caynes, readers gain a front-row seat to the evolution of an ordinary individual becoming an extraordinary force for change. Uncovering the challenges, sacrifices, and triumphs along the way, "The Unmasked" paints a vivid portrait of Caynes's tireless efforts to expose internet trolls and protect vulnerable victims.

As the book unravels, it exposes the disturbing realities of online abuse, shedding light on the profound impact it has on individuals, families, and communities. Through Damian Charles Caynes's tireless work, readers witness firsthand how one person can make a genuine difference in a rapidly evolving digital landscape.

"The Unmasked" invites readers to explore the intricate mindset of trolls, unveiling their motivations, tactics, and the lasting damage they inflict. With each chapter, Caynes's journey becomes increasingly enthralling, as he unapologetically battles against the forces of anonymity and cruelty that plague social media platforms.

Ultimately, "The Unmasked" serves as an inspiring testament to the power of conviction and the strength of human compassion. It challenges readers to confront the dark side of the internet while offering hope that through resilience and determination, we can create a safer and more inclusive online environment for all.

Introduction to Damian Charles Caynes:

Damian Charles Caynes's journey as an unlikely hero begins with his early life and upbringing. Born in a small town, Caynes had a relatively ordinary childhood, filled with typical experiences and challenges. However, it was his encounters with the internet that would shape his character and set him on a path towards becoming a formidable force against online abuse.

As a young adult, Caynes discovered the vast potential of the internet for connection and information. It fascinated him how people from different backgrounds and cultures could come together in online communities, sharing ideas and experiences. The internet became his window into a world beyond the confines of his small town.

Unfortunately, Caynes also witnessed the darker side of the internet. He encountered trolls, individuals who derived pleasure from harassing and tormenting others. These trolls unleashed vitriolic attacks on innocent people, causing unimaginable pain and suffering behind the cloak of anonymity.

These experiences deeply affected Caynes, stirring within him a sense of injustice and a burning desire to protect those targeted by online abuse. What began as a personal fascination with the internet soon transformed into a relentless determination to combat this growing problem.

Caynes's initial encounters with trolls made him realize that he couldn't simply be a passive observer. He needed to educate himself about the tactics used by trolls and understand their motivations. This led him down a path of extensive research, learning about the psychology of trolls and exploring strategies to counter their harmful actions.

In this prologue, we glimpse into Damian Charles Caynes's early life and his formative experiences with the internet. We witness the spark of curiosity and empathy that ignited within him, laying the foundation for his extraordinary journey as a troll hunter. Join us as we delve deeper into his story, uncovering the challenges, triumphs, and profound impact Caynes has had in combating online abuse.

Prologue: An Unlikely Hero Emerges

In this section, we delve into the early life and experiences of Damian Charles Caynes, the protagonist of our story. Born and raised in a small town, Caynes led a relatively typical life until the advent of the internet changed everything.

As a young adult, Caynes found solace and excitement in online communities. These virtual spaces offered a sense of belonging and connection that was often lacking in Caynes's physical surroundings. It was within these online communities that he discovered both the immense potential for positive interaction and the darker side of the internet.

Enter the trolls – individuals who derived pleasure from sowing discord, stoking negativity, and inflicting harm on others. Caynes's first encounters with these internet trolls were bewildering and deeply troubling. He witnessed firsthand the power they held to disrupt communities, spread vitriol, and prey upon unsuspecting individuals.

These experiences left an indelible mark on Caynes's worldview and ignited a fierce determination within him. He became acutely aware of the destructive impact trolls had on the lives of their victims and the toxic culture they fostered online. It was here that Damian Charles Caynes's journey as a troll killer began.

Through his initial encounters with trolls, Caynes recognized that he possessed the unique ability to peer into the darkness of their minds and understand their motivations. This insight fueled his desire to confront these malevolent individuals head-on and protect those subjected to their abuse.

As we embark on this extraordinary journey with Damian Charles Caynes, we will witness his transformation from an ordinary individual into an unexpected hero in the fight against online abuse. We will follow his relentless pursuit of justice, uncovering the challenges, sacrifices, and triumphs he encounters along the way.

So join us as we dive into "The Unmasked: The Untold Journey of Damian Charles Caynes, The Troll Killer," and discover how one person's unwavering commitment can make a genuine difference in combating online harassment. Together, let us shed light on the dark corners of the internet and bring hope to those who have suffered at the hands of trolls.

The catalyst for Damian Charles Caynes's transformation into a tireless advocate against online abuse can be traced back to a pivotal moment or incident that deeply impacted him. This event served as a wake-up call, igniting his passion for fighting the trolls that plague the internet.

This particular incident left an indelible mark on Caynes, stirring up a whirlwind of emotions within him. It struck him on a personal level, exposing him to the devastating consequences that online abuse can have on its victims. The emotional toll it took on him was profound, filling him with a profound sense of injustice and a burning desire to take action.

What transpired during this catalyst moment motivated Caynes to embark on a relentless journey to combat online harassment. He realized the urgent need for someone to stand up against the forces of anonymity and cruelty that hide behind the digital mask of trolls. It was in this moment that Caynes made a conscious choice to dedicate himself to challenging and shining a light on this dark corner of the internet.

The catalyst not only propelled Caynes into action but also shaped his unique perspective and unwavering determination in his fight against online abuse. It was an unexpected turning point in his life, leading him down a path he never anticipated but one that he felt called to follow.

As we delve deeper into Damian Charles Caynes's remarkable journey, we will uncover the defining moments and experiences that have molded him into an unassuming hero. We will witness firsthand the impacts of his work and learn how one person can make a genuine difference in combatting online harassment.

Join us as we embark on this extraordinary journey with Damian Charles Caynes—a journey that will expose the disturbing realities of online abuse, challenge societal norms, and offer hope for a safer and more compassionate digital world.

AS DAMIAN CHARLES CAYNES delved deeper into the realm of the internet, his eyes were opened to the widespread prevalence of online harassment. What once seemed like an innocuous playground for connection and information now revealed a darker underbelly filled with trolls and malicious behavior.

Driven by an unwavering sense of justice, Caynes dedicated himself to understanding the scope and severity of this issue. He embarked on a journey of research, seeking out knowledge and strategies to combat trolls and protect vulnerable individuals from their harm.

Through countless hours of study and exploration, Caynes became well-versed in the tactics employed by trolls and the devastating effects they had on their victims. He saw firsthand the emotional toll taken on those who fell prey to the relentless attacks of these anonymous tormentors.

With each revelation, Caynes's determination grew stronger. He recognized the urgent need for action and began strategizing ways to confront and expose online abusers. He immersed himself in the intricacies of troll psychology, studying their motivations and methods. This deep understanding allowed him to formulate effective approaches to counter their toxic behavior.

As Caynes developed purpose and determination in his mission, he sought out allies who shared his passion for combating online abuse. Collaborating with like-minded individuals, he engaged in discussions and brainstormed innovative ideas to disrupt the control trolls held over their victims.

Through tireless dedication and ceaseless research, Caynes honed his skills and expanded his knowledge base. A strong foundation was laid for his future endeavors, setting the stage for the heroic acts that would follow.

But this chapter in Caynes's journey is only the beginning. The challenges he faces are immense, as trolls continue to plague the online world with their cruelty. Yet with an unyielding resolve and a growing arsenal of strategies, Damian Charles Caynes is prepared to take on this battle head-on. In the chapters to come, we will witness his evolution from an unlikely hero to a towering force against internet trolls.

Join us as we delve deeper into the incredible journey of Damian Charles Caynes, The Troll Killer, and uncover the remarkable ways in which he fights for justice in the digital landscape. Together, we will learn from his experiences, gain insights into the mindset of trolls, and discover how one person can make a genuine difference in creating a safer online environment for all.

As we delve into the captivating journey of Damian Charles Caynes, it becomes evident that his transformation from an ordinary individual to an unexpected advocate against online abuse is nothing short of remarkable. Caynes's story is a testament to the power of one person's determination and the profound impact they can have in combating internet trolls.

Throughout his early experiences on the internet, Caynes found himself drawn into various online communities, exploring the vast potential for connection and communication. Little did he know that within these virtual spaces, he would encounter a dark side lurking beneath the surface – the world of internet trolls.

It was a defining moment, a catalyst that ignited Caynes's passion to fight against online abuse. Witnessing firsthand the destructive behavior of trolls and its effect on individuals, Caynes felt compelled to take action. The emotional toll this realization took on him fueled his determination to make a difference.

With purpose and unwavering determination, Caynes set out on a journey of researching, learning, and strategizing ways to combat trolls. He sought to understand their motives, tactics, and the devastating consequences they inflict upon their victims. Through this process, Caynes emerged as an unexpected hero in the fight against online harassment.

Teasing readers with hints of what lies ahead, Caynes's transformation is just the beginning of an extraordinary journey. His impact in this fight against internet trolls will leave an indelible mark on our understanding of online abuse and the steps we can take to create a safer digital landscape.

Join us as we embark on this enthralling narrative, exploring the defining moments and experiences that shaped Damian Charles Caynes into the unassuming hero known as "The Troll Killer." Let us discover how one individual's resilience and determination can truly make a difference in combating the forces of anonymity and cruelty that plague social media platforms.

Chapter One: The Birth of an Internet Warrior

Damian Charles Caynes's journey as an internet warrior was ignited by his early experiences with the internet and his fascination with online communities. From the moment he first ventured into cyberspace, Caynes was captivated by the vast possibilities it offered for connection, knowledge, and self-expression.

As a young internet user, Caynes experienced the excitement of connecting with people from all around the world, exchanging ideas, and exploring different perspectives. The internet became a gateway to new worlds and a source of endless fascination for him. He found solace in the anonymity and freedom that the online realm provided, allowing him to express himself more openly and authentically.

However, amidst the vastness of the digital landscape, Caynes soon encountered a darker side - the trolls. These individuals, motivated by a desire to provoke, harass, and spread negativity, left an indelible mark on Caynes's psyche. Their taunts, insults, and relentless attacks on innocent individuals opened his eyes to the inherent dangers lurking in cyberspace.

These early encounters with trolls deeply affected Caynes, igniting a growing determination within him to take a stand against online abuse. He witnessed firsthand the devastating impact that these faceless tormentors had on their victims, and it struck a chord deep within his empathetic soul. Caynes felt compelled to fight back, to protect those who were being targeted and to restore decency and civility to online communities.

Motivated by a sense of justice and an unwavering commitment to combatting online abuse, Caynes embarked on a journey that would define both his life and purpose. In these early days, he dedicated endless hours to researching and understanding the psychology behind trolling behavior. He delved into the minds of trolls, attempting to grasp their motivations and tactics in order to develop strategies for countering their harmful actions.

Through his exploration of online spaces, Damian Charles Caynes began to understand the power dynamics at play between trolls and their victims. He recognized that trolls thrived on anonymity, using it as a shield to perpetrate their toxic behavior without consequence. This realization fueled Caynes's determination not only to unmask trolls but also to expose the broader societal issues that allowed such abuse to persist.

Caynes's early efforts focused on creating awareness within his immediate circles about the dangers of online harassment. He engaged in conversations with friends, family members, and fellow internet users, shedding light on the detrimental effects of trolling and urging them to become more responsible digital citizens. His passion for combating online abuse grew stronger with each conversation, motivating him to expand his reach and amplify his message.

As Damian Charles Caynes's chapter as an internet warrior unfolded, he embarked on a mission shaped by his early experiences with the internet. His dedication to fighting online abuse was born from a desire to protect others from the same pain and suffering he had witnessed. With each step, he grew closer to becoming the unassuming hero known as "The Troll Killer," driven by an unwavering commitment to making the digital world safer for all who inhabit it.

As we delve deeper into Damian Charles Caynes's extraordinary journey as an internet warrior, we will explore the emergence of trolls and how their effect on Caynes's mindset propelled him towards action. Join us as we uncover the challenges he faced along the way and celebrate his early successes that fueled his determination in Chapter One: The Birth of an Internet Warrior.

INTRODUCE THE CONCEPT of trolling and its evolution within online spaces. Discuss how the emergence of trolls affected Damian Charles Caynes's mindset and shaped his desire to combat online abuse.

Trolling, in the context of the internet, refers to the act of deliberately provoking or harassing others online by posting inflammatory or offensive comments. The term "troll" originated from early internet culture, where individuals would purposefully disrupt online communities to elicit strong reactions from other users.

For Damian Charles Caynes, encountering trolls for the first time was a startling experience that left a lasting impression. These encounters exposed him to the darker side of the internet, introducing him to the harmful effects of online abuse on individuals and communities.

The emotional and psychological impact of these interactions played a significant role in shaping Caynes's mindset. He witnessed firsthand the pain, humiliation, and distress caused by trolls' malicious words and actions. This ignited a deep sense of empathy and compassion within him, compelling him to take a stand against online abuse.

Caynes understood that behind every offensive comment or hurtful message was a real person on the receiving end. This realization fueled his determination to protect others from the harmful effects of trolling and foster a safer and more inclusive digital environment.

The encounters with trolls awakened a sense of responsibility in Caynes. He recognized that simply ignoring or dismissing their behavior perpetuated a cycle of harm. Instead, he chose to confront this issue head-on, driven by a belief that everyone deserves to feel safe and respected online.

As Caynes's awareness of the prevalence and severity of online abuse grew, so did his resolve to fight against it. Armed with empathy, knowledge, and an unwavering commitment to justice, Damian Charles Caynes began his remarkable journey as an internet warrior, determined to make a difference in the world of trolling.

Caynes's growing determination to combat online abuse was fueled by a series of pivotal moments and personal experiences that solidified his commitment to fighting against trolls. These moments acted as a catalyst for Caynes, propelling him into action and inspiring him to make a difference in the world of online harassment.

One significant factor that led to Caynes's decision to actively engage in battling trolls was his deep sense of empathy. As he witnessed the devastating impact that online abuse had on its victims, Caynes felt an overwhelming desire to help and protect those who were targeted. This empathy was further intensified by his own encounters with trolls and the emotional toll it took on him personally.

These early experiences served as a wake-up call for Caynes, revealing the extent of the problem and the urgent need for action. Recognizing the powerlessness felt by many victims, he decided to take matters into his own hands and become their advocate. Caynes believed that no one should have to endure the pain and suffering caused by online harassment and became determined to use his skills and platform to combat this pervasive issue.

In his initial steps to address online abuse, Caynes focused on raising awareness about the problem. He educated himself about the various forms of trolling and studied the tactics employed by trolls to manipulate and harass their victims. Armed with this knowledge, Caynes developed strategies to counteract these tactics and empower those who were being targeted.

One of the key strategies Caynes adopted was providing support and resources to victims of online abuse. He created online communities where individuals could share their stories, find solidarity, and access guidance on how to deal with trolls effectively. Caynes also sought out partnerships with like-minded organizations that shared his mission, amplifying his reach and impact.

Additionally, Caynes recognized the importance of educating individuals about responsible online behavior and digital literacy. He started organizing workshops, seminars, and awareness campaigns in schools, workplaces, and community centers. By teaching people how to navigate the online world safely and responsibly, Caynes aimed to prevent trolling behavior from escalating and creating a more inclusive online environment.

As time went on, Caynes's strategies evolved and grew more sophisticated. He began engaging directly with trolls, using their own tactics against them to expose their true identities and hold them accountable for their actions. Caynes's investigative work often involved collaborating with other internet users who shared his passion for justice.

Overall, Caynes's early journey in combatting online abuse was marked by a deepening determination to make a difference in the lives of those affected by trolling. His commitment led him to develop innovative strategies, collaborate with like-minded individuals, and passionately educate others about the importance of standing up against online harassment. With each step he took, Caynes moved closer towards becoming an empowered warrior in the fight against internet trolls.

During his journey to fight against online abuse, Damian Charles Caynes encountered numerous challenges and obstacles. These difficulties presented themselves in both online and offline forms, testing Caynes's determination and resolve.

One of the main challenges Caynes faced was the resistance and skepticism from individuals and communities who were unaware or dismissive of the extent of the problem. Many people failed to recognize the severity and significance of online abuse, dismissing it as trivial or inconsequential. This lack of understanding made Caynes's mission even more difficult, as he had to tirelessly educate others about the harmful effects of trolling and the urgent need to combat it.

Additionally, Caynes encountered setbacks and failures along the way. As with any endeavor, there were moments when things did not go as planned or expected. Some of Caynes's early strategies to combat trolls may not have yielded the desired results, leading him to reassess his approach and learn from these experiences. These setbacks served as valuable learning opportunities for Caynes, allowing him to refine his methods and develop more effective strategies.

Despite these challenges and setbacks, Caynes remained undeterred in his mission to fight against online abuse. He recognized that change takes time and persistence, and he was willing to adapt and evolve in order to make a difference. Rather than becoming discouraged, Caynes used these challenges as fuel to further propel his efforts forward.

By facing these obstacles head-on, Damian Charles Caynes demonstrated his resilience and unwavering commitment to his cause. Through his determination and willingness to learn from setbacks, Caynes was able to overcome challenges and continue making progress in combating online abuse. His journey serves as an inspiration to all those who face adversity in their pursuit of justice and creating a safer digital environment for all.

Note: The content above has been written in a third-person perspective, focusing on the subject matter rather than the interaction with the reader.

Early in his journey, Damian Charles Caynes experienced a series of significant accomplishments that fueled his dedication to combating trolls and online abuse. These early successes validated Caynes's mission and served as powerful motivators for him to continue his fight.

One such accomplishment was when Caynes successfully exposed a particularly notorious troll who had been terrorizing multiple individuals online. Through his meticulous investigative work and collaboration with other internet users, Caynes was able to uncover the true identity of the troll and bring their actions to light. This not only provided a sense of justice for the victims but also served as a warning to other trolls that they could no longer hide behind the veil of anonymity.

Another notable success for Caynes was when he launched a campaign to raise awareness about the impact of online abuse on mental health. By sharing compelling stories of individuals who had been deeply affected by trolling, Caynes was able to garner significant media attention and support from a wide range of people. This increased visibility helped to amplify the message that online abuse should not be tolerated and spurred others to join the fight against trolls.

As these victories accumulated, Caynes's identity as an internet warrior began to take shape. The positive outcomes of his efforts reaffirmed his belief in the importance of combating online abuse and further motivated him to continue pushing forward. These early successes also provided Caynes with valuable insights and strategies that would prove instrumental in his future battles against trolls.

It is through these early experiences and achievements that Damian Charles Caynes's determination and passion for fighting online abuse were solidified. The victories he achieved not only validated his mission but also propelled him towards becoming an influential figure in the fight against internet trolls. With each triumph, Caynes grew more resolute in his commitment to creating a safer and more inclusive online environment for all.

Chapter Two: A World of Shadows

The dark side of the internet is a vast and eerie realm where trolling culture thrives. It is a world of shadows that many internet users are unaware of, but one that can have far-reaching consequences. In this chapter, we will explore the origins and evolution of trolling, from its harmless beginnings as pranks to its transformation into malicious and harmful behavior.

Trolling refers to the act of intentionally provoking and harassing others online for personal amusement or satisfaction. It has been around since the early days of the internet, but with the rise of social media and online anonymity, trolling has become more prevalent and sophisticated. Trolls hide behind screen names and avatars, which allows them to operate without fear of consequences or accountability.

The anonymity granted by the online world has dire consequences for victims of trolling. Without the fear of being identified, trolls feel emboldened to unleash their toxic behavior on unsuspecting individuals. They revel in the power they wield over others, delighting in the pain and distress they cause. The consequences for victims can be severe, ranging from emotional distress and mental health issues to reputational damage and even physical harm.

One of the most insidious aspects of trolling is its impact on online communities. Trolls disrupt conversations, derail discussions, and create an atmosphere of hostility and toxicity. They thrive on chaos and conflict, sowing discord wherever they go. This behavior hinders constructive dialogue and prevents the formation of genuine connections between internet users.

The toll on victims of trolling cannot be understated. They are subjected to relentless attacks on their character, appearance, beliefs, and even their personal lives. The psychological and emotional impact can be devastating, leading to feelings of helplessness, depression, and anxiety. Victims often find it challenging to cope with the constant barrage of abuse, and many suffer in silence due to shame or fear of further harassment.

Addressing the issue of anonymity is crucial in combating trolling behavior. While privacy is important on the internet, allowing individuals to hide behind false identities facilitates a culture of impunity for trolls. Striking a balance between privacy and accountability is a complex task, but one that must be undertaken to protect internet users from the harmful effects of trolling.

In the next sections of this chapter, we will delve deeper into the motivations behind trolling behavior and explore the psychological factors that contribute to its prevalence. We will also examine real-life examples of the impact that trolls have on individuals and communities alike. By shining a light on this dark corner of the internet, we hope to raise awareness about the need for action against trolls and create a safer online environment for all.

DELVING INTO THE PSYCHOLOGY and motivations behind trolling behavior provides valuable insights into the complex world of online harassment. While it may be tempting to dismiss trolls as mere troublemakers seeking attention, their motivations run deeper than that. Uncovering these underlying factors is crucial to understanding why trolls engage in such harmful activities.

One primary motivation behind trolling is the desire for power and control. Trolls often feel powerless in their own lives or face challenges that diminish their self-esteem. By targeting others online, they can assert dominance and exert control over their victims. This power dynamic allows trolls to experience a sense of superiority and satisfaction that may be lacking in their offline lives.

Attention-seeking is another key motivation for trolls. Many individuals who engage in trolling activities crave visibility and recognition. They thrive on the reactions and responses they elicit from their victims and the wider online community. Negative attention, such as outrage or anger, serves as validation for their actions, reinforcing their belief that they have successfully disrupted someone's life or caused distress.

Inflicting harm on others can also be a motivating factor for trolls. Some trolls derive pleasure from causing emotional pain and suffering to their victims. This sadistic tendency may stem from unresolved personal issues or a lack of empathy towards others. The anonymity provided by the internet allows them to detach themselves from the consequences of their actions, enabling them to engage in acts of cruelty without facing accountability.

It's important to note that not all trolls share the same motivations or mindset. The reasons behind trolling can vary greatly from one individual to another. Personal experiences, such as past trauma or instances of victimization, may play a significant role in shaping a person's behavior online. Additionally, certain online environments or communities can foster a culture that encourages trolling, further fueling individuals' motivations.

Understanding these underlying motivations can help society develop effective strategies for combatting online harassment. By addressing the root causes of trolling behavior, we can implement targeted interventions that aim to change attitudes and behaviors. Empathy-building initiatives, educational programs, and community-led efforts can all contribute to creating a more respectful and inclusive online environment.

In conclusion, delving into the psychology and motivations behind trolling sheds light on why individuals engage in such harmful behavior online. Factors such as the desire for power, attention-seeking, and the need to inflict harm contribute to this destructive activity. By understanding these motivations, we can take steps towards reducing online harassment and fostering a safer digital landscape for all users.

THE IMPACT OF TROLLS extends far beyond their online targets, reaching into the very fabric of society. Through their disruptive and harmful behavior, trolls leave a trail of emotional distress, mental health issues, reputational damage, and even physical harm in their wake.

Real-life examples vividly illustrate the profound consequences of trolling. Victims often experience intense emotional distress, including feelings of fear, anxiety, depression, and isolation. The relentless onslaught of abusive messages and relentless harassment can take a severe toll on their mental well-being, leading to long-lasting psychological trauma.

In addition to the personal impact on individuals, trolls also have a detrimental effect on communities and broader society. Online spaces that were once vibrant hubs for constructive discussions are hijacked by trolls, who thrive on sowing discord, spreading misinformation, and stifling meaningful conversations. This hinders the exchange of ideas and can prevent important social issues from being addressed effectively.

Furthermore, trolls create an environment of fear and intimidation, silencing voices and deterring individuals from participating in online discourse. They discourage open dialogue and discourage people from expressing themselves freely, leading to a chilling effect on freedom of speech.

Beyond the psychological and social consequences, trolls can also cause significant reputational damage. By launching smear campaigns or spreading false information about their victims, they tarnish their online presence and credibility. This can have real-world repercussions, impacting employment prospects, personal relationships, and overall self-esteem.

In some cases, trolling escalates beyond the digital realm and spills into the physical world. Threats of violence or harm made by trolls can instill genuine fear in their targets. This not only poses a direct risk to individuals but also erodes the sense of safety within communities as a whole.

By disrupting online communities and hindering constructive discussions, trolls impede progress and prevent meaningful change from taking place. Their actions perpetuate division and negativity, making it difficult for individuals to come together to address pressing issues and find common ground.

It is crucial to recognize the profound impact that trolling behavior has on individuals, communities, and society as a whole. By shedding light on these consequences, we can begin to understand the urgency of combating this pervasive issue and work towards creating a safer and more inclusive online environment for everyone.

THE TOLL ON VICTIMS of online abuse inflicted by trolls is devastating and far-reaching. Countless individuals have experienced the psychological, emotional, and social impacts of this form of harassment. Their stories serve as powerful reminders of the harmful effects that trolling can have on people's lives.

One victim, Sarah, found herself targeted by a relentless troll who bombarded her with hateful messages and threats. As a result, Sarah's self-esteem plummeted, and she developed anxiety and depression. The constant fear of being attacked online made her withdraw from social interactions and lose trust in others. Seeking justice seemed like an uphill battle, as the troll hid behind fake accounts and maintained their anonymity.

Another victim, Mark, became the subject of relentless cyberbullying after expressing his opinion on a controversial topic. The online attacks soon spilled over into his personal life, with the troll contacting his employer and spreading false rumors about him. Mark felt isolated and ashamed, unable to escape the constant harassment even when he tried to disconnect from the internet. His struggle to find support was met with skepticism and indifference, exacerbating his feelings of helplessness.

These examples illustrate just a fraction of the experiences endured by victims of trolling. Individuals subjected to such abuse often face challenges in seeking justice due to the anonymous nature of online harassment. Identifying and holding trolls accountable can be a complex and time-consuming process that requires collaboration between victims, law enforcement agencies, and online platforms.

Finding support can also be an arduous journey for victims. Many feel ostracized or blamed for their own victimization, causing them to suffer in silence. Establishing a strong support system that understands the unique aspects of online abuse is crucial for victims' healing and recovery.

Reclaiming one's online presence can be another significant hurdle for victims. The fear of being targeted again may lead them to abandon or limit their online activities, resulting in isolation and missed opportunities for connection and self-expression. Empowering victims to regain control over their digital lives requires comprehensive strategies that address both the practical and psychological aspects of rebuilding their online presence.

By shedding light on the toll that trolling takes on its victims, we gain a deeper understanding of the urgency and importance of combating this pervasive issue. Through awareness, education, and collective action, we can work towards creating a safer online environment where individuals can express themselves freely without fear of harassment or harm.

THE BATTLE AGAINST anonymity plays a fundamental role in enabling trolling behavior and creating an environment conducive to abuse. In this chapter, we will delve into the debates surrounding internet privacy versus accountability in relation to combating online harassment. We will explore potential strategies for reducing anonymity and increasing transparency to mitigate the negative effects of trolling.

Anonymity on the internet provides a shield for trolls, allowing them to operate freely without fear of repercussions. It gives them a sense of power and protection, emboldening their harmful actions. However, this very anonymity is also what makes it difficult to hold them accountable for their behavior. Identifying trolls and taking legal or social action against them becomes challenging when their true identities are hidden.

One strategy to combat anonymity is through increased transparency. Platforms can implement stricter identification protocols, such as verifying user identities or requiring users to link their accounts to real-world information. This would make it easier to track down and report trolls, making them think twice before engaging in abusive behavior. Additionally, platforms can provide more comprehensive reporting mechanisms that allow victims to submit evidence of abuse anonymously if needed.

Another approach involves fostering a culture of accountability within online communities. By promoting responsible behavior and encouraging users to take ownership of their actions, we can create an atmosphere where trolls are less likely to thrive. Providing clear guidelines and enforcing strict moderation policies can help maintain a respectful and safe online environment.

However, it is essential to balance these efforts with the need for privacy on the internet. Anonymity can be vital for whistleblowers, activists, and individuals who require protection from potential harm. Therefore, any strategies aimed at reducing anonymity must be carefully implemented to preserve privacy rights.

Education and awareness also play a crucial role in addressing the challenges posed by anonymity. By educating internet users about the consequences of online harassment and the impact it has on individuals and communities, we can foster a collective responsibility to combat trolling behavior. Teaching digital literacy skills and promoting empathy and respect online can empower individuals to protect themselves and others from abuse.

In conclusion, the battle against anonymity is a complex issue that requires careful consideration. While reducing anonymity may help mitigate trolling's negative effects, it must be done without sacrificing privacy rights or stifling legitimate forms of expression. By implementing stricter identification protocols, fostering accountability within online communities, and prioritizing education and awareness, we can create a safer online environment for all users.

Chapter Three: The First Encounter

Damian Charles Caynes's first encounter with a troll was a pivotal moment that prompted him to take a stand against online abuse. This specific incident acted as the catalyst for his unwavering determination to combat trolls and protect their victims.

When Damian Charles Caynes first encountered a troll, he was taken aback by the cruelty and vitriol directed at innocent individuals. The troll's hurtful and malicious comments ignited a range of emotions within Caynes, including anger, frustration, and empathy for those being targeted. Witnessing the devastating impact of online harassment firsthand, Caynes was driven to make a difference and fight against this pervasive issue.

This initial confrontation with a troll solidified Caynes's commitment to combating online abuse. He recognized the urgent need to protect vulnerable individuals from the emotional and psychological harm caused by trolls. Determined to create a safer environment on the internet, Caynes vowed to expose these tormentors and bring them to justice.

The emotional toll of this first encounter served as a powerful motivator for Caynes. It fueled his resolve to stand up against trolls and offer support to their victims. Understanding the profound impact that online abuse can have on individuals, Caynes became even more dedicated to fighting for their rights and well-being.

However, this journey was not without its challenges. Confronting trolls meant facing resistance and pushback from both the trolls themselves and supporters of anonymity. Caynes encountered skepticism from individuals who dismissed online harassment as inconsequential or trivial. Nonetheless, he remained undeterred, willing to endure personal sacrifices and risks in order to protect those affected by trolls.

This first encounter with a troll taught Damian Charles Caynes invaluable lessons about the nature of online abuse. It provided him with a deeper understanding of trolls' motivations and tactics, informing his evolving perspective on how best to combat them. As he moved forward in his mission, Caynes would use these insights to refine his strategies and develop new approaches.

In conclusion, Damian Charles Caynes's first encounter with a troll was a transformative experience that shaped his determination to combat online abuse. This emotional confrontation acted as a catalyst for his unwavering commitment to protect victims and dismantle the toxic culture of trolling. Through this chapter, readers gain insight into the defining moments that launched Caynes into his extraordinary journey as an internet warrior.

In Chapter Three of "The Unmasked: The Untold Journey of Damian Charles Caynes, The Troll Killer," readers are introduced to the strategies employed by Caynes to combat online abuse. After his initial confrontation with a troll, Caynes is determined to take a stand against these malicious individuals and protect their victims.

Caynes begins by utilizing various approaches and techniques to address the issue of trolling. He understands that engaging in direct confrontations can sometimes fuel trolls and perpetuate their behavior. Instead, he focuses on reporting abusive content and supporting those who have been targeted. By flagging offensive posts and reporting them to the relevant social media platforms, Caynes aims to get trolls' harmful content removed and hold them accountable for their actions.

In this chapter, we explore whether these strategies were successful in dealing with the specific troll encountered by Caynes. While it may take time for platforms to respond and take action, Caynes remains persistent in his efforts to combat online abuse. He understands that even if he cannot eliminate trolling altogether, he can make a difference by amplifying victims' voices and providing support.

Throughout his early encounters, Caynes learns valuable lessons that shape his approach in fighting online harassment. He recognizes the importance of creating awareness and educating others about the impact of trolling. By informing individuals about the consequences of online abuse and highlighting its harmful effects, he hopes to discourage potential trolls and empower victims.

It should be noted that Caynes's journey to combat trolls is an ongoing process, with new challenges emerging along the way. While some strategies may prove successful in dealing with certain trolls, others may require different approaches. Nonetheless, each encounter serves as a learning experience for Caynes, solidifying his commitment to protecting vulnerable individuals from online harm.

As "The Unmasked" continues, readers will witness the evolution of Caynes's strategies and tactics as he confronts increasingly complex situations. Each chapter delves deeper into the fight against internet trolls and showcases Caynes's unwavering determination to create a safer online environment for all.

Stay tuned for the upcoming chapters as Caynes's journey unfolds, shedding light on the critical role he plays in exposing trolls and advocating for justice in the digital realm.

THE FIRST ENCOUNTER with a troll had a profound personal impact on Damian Charles Caynes. It was an emotional experience that stirred a range of feelings within him, including anger, frustration, and empathy. This initial confrontation acted as a catalyst for Caynes's decision to take a stand against online abuse.

As Caynes grappled with the aftermath of this encounter, he found himself experiencing heightened awareness and motivation. The realization of the severity and prevalence of online harassment fueled his determination to combat trolls and protect their victims. This first encounter served as a wake-up call, solidifying Caynes's commitment to making a difference in the world of internet trolls.

However, the personal impact of the first encounter also led Caynes to question his chosen path. He faced numerous challenges and obstacles along the way, both online and offline. There were moments when he questioned whether his efforts were making a meaningful impact or if they were merely a drop in the ocean of online abuse.

Despite these doubts, Caynes's resolve remained steadfast. The first encounter with a troll revealed the disturbing realities of online harassment and compelled him to fight even harder. It became clear to him that addressing this issue was not just a personal mission but a moral obligation.

This chapter sets the stage for future developments in Caynes's journey. It lays the foundation for the strategies he will employ and the lessons he will learn as he continues to confront trolls head-on. The first encounter serves as a crucial turning point, shaping his evolving perspective on trolls and solidifying his commitment to combating online abuse.

As readers delve deeper into "The Unmasked," they will witness Caynes's unwavering determination and resilience as he battles against the forces of anonymity and cruelty that plague social media platforms. Through his journey, we explore the intricate mindset of trolls, shed light on the profound impact of online abuse, and ultimately find hope in the power of conviction and human compassion.

Join us as we continue Damian Charles Caynes's untold journey—a journey that exposes the dark side of the internet while offering hope for a safer and more inclusive online environment for all.

As Damian Charles Caynes embarked on his mission to combat online abuse, he encountered a myriad of challenges and obstacles along the way. From trolls themselves to supporters of anonymity and dismissive attitudes towards online harassment, Caynes faced significant resistance in his quest for justice.

One of the primary challenges Caynes faced was the direct opposition from trolls themselves. These individuals, hiding behind the veil of anonymity, wielded their keyboards as weapons, launching relentless attacks on their victims. They retaliated against any attempt to expose their true identities or hold them accountable for their actions. Caynes found himself locked in a constant battle of wits, trying to outsmart and overcome these cunning adversaries.

In addition to the trolls themselves, Caynes also faced resistance from those who supported the notion of anonymity on the internet. Some argued that it was an essential part of freedom of speech and expression, making it difficult for Caynes to convince them of the harm caused by online harassment. It required immense patience and persuasion to change minds and gain support for his cause.

Furthermore, there were individuals who dismissively viewed online harassment as inconsequential or trivial. They failed to recognize the profound impact trolling could have on its victims' mental health, self-esteem, and overall well-being. Overcoming this dismissiveness and raising awareness about the severity of online abuse became another obstacle for Caynes to surmount.

Taking a stand against trolls came with significant personal sacrifices and risks. Caynes put his own reputation on the line as he exposed trolls and their harmful behaviors. He faced backlash, threats, and even attempts to tarnish his credibility. Yet, he remained steadfast in his commitment to combat online abuse, refusing to be silenced by those who sought to protect trolls at all costs.

Throughout this chapter, readers will witness firsthand the challenges and obstacles that Caynes encountered in his early encounters with trolls. They will gain insight into the resistance he faced from trolls themselves, supporters of anonymity, and those who dismissed online harassment as inconsequential. By examining these challenges, readers begin to understand the magnitude of Caynes's determination and the uphill battle he faced in his relentless pursuit of justice.

Stay tuned as we delve further into Damian Charles Caynes's journey and explore how these initial challenges shaped his evolving perspectives on online abuse and troll hunting.

Reflecting on the key takeaways from Damian Charles Caynes's first confrontation with a troll, we gain insight into how this experience shapes his evolving perspective on online abuse. This pivotal encounter serves as a turning point in Caynes's journey, solidifying his commitment to combatting trolls and protecting their victims.

As Damian engages with the troll during this initial confrontation, he begins to unravel the tactics and motivations behind their abusive behavior. Through direct engagement, he gains a deeper understanding of the impact that online abuse has on its victims. This newfound knowledge fuels his determination to take a stand against trolls and seek justice for those affected.

The first encounter also highlights the challenges and obstacles faced by Caynes in his mission to combat online abuse. Trolls often relish anonymity and employ various tactics to evade identification or consequences. Caynes experiences firsthand the resistance faced from trolls themselves, as well as from supporters of anonymity who dismiss online harassment as inconsequential. Despite these adversities, Damian remains resolute and becomes even more determined to shine a light on the dark corners of the internet.

This early experience serves as a stepping stone for Caynes's future efforts. It shapes his strategies for combating trolls, honing his ability to identify their tactics and motivations. As he delves deeper into his mission, Caynes's understanding of trolls evolves, enabling him to refine his approach in effectively exposing them.

Looking ahead, this chapter sets the stage for Caynes's continued fight against internet trolls. It establishes a foundation of resilience and determination as he navigates the complex landscape of online abuse. With each subsequent encounter, Caynes learns and grows, further bolstering his commitment to protect vulnerable individuals from the harm inflicted by trolls.

In conclusion, the first encounter between Damian Charles Caynes and a troll marks a significant turning point in his journey. Lessons learned from this experience shape his evolving perspective on online abuse and provide valuable insights into trolls' motivations and tactics. This chapter lays the groundwork for Caynes's unwavering commitment to expose and combat trolls in future chapters, driving him to make a genuine difference in the fight against online harassment.

Chapter Four: Stepping into the Fray

Caynes's decision to actively engage in battling trolls and seeking justice for their victims was driven by a combination of internal struggles and motivations. Deeply affected by the online abuse he witnessed, Caynes felt an overwhelming sense of responsibility to make a difference in the lives of those targeted by trolls.

Motivated by a strong sense of justice, Caynes recognized the magnitude of the problem and had an unwavering resolve to confront it head-on. He understood that online harassment had significant and lasting effects on individuals, families, and communities. This understanding fueled his determination to challenge the status quo and create a safer digital environment.

Caynes's realization that he could be a catalyst for change encouraged him to step up and take action. He recognized that he possessed unique skills, experiences, and insights that could make a genuine impact in combating online abuse. With an empathetic heart and a genuine desire to protect vulnerable victims, Caynes dedicated himself to this cause.

His decision to actively engage in battling trolls was not without its challenges and obstacles. As he began his mission, Caynes encountered legal barriers and faced resistance from trolls who sought to silence him. However, these challenges only served to strengthen his resolve and determination.

Caynes knew that his commitment to fighting online abuse would require personal sacrifices. He understood the risks involved in challenging powerful individuals hiding behind anonymity. Despite the emotional toll it took on his mental well-being, Caynes remained steadfast in his pursuit of justice.

Early successes in exposing trolls and bringing them to justice validated Caynes's efforts and solidified his commitment to his mission. Each victory gave him renewed hope and bolstered his motivation to continue his fight against online harassment.

Alongside these successes, Caynes also experienced setbacks. These failures became valuable learning opportunities for him, teaching him the importance of adaptability and resilience. Throughout these early experiences, Caynes honed his strategies for combating online abuse, continuously evolving his tactics to stay one step ahead of trolls.

Lessons learned from Caynes's early encounters with trolls and victims shaped his approach moving forward. These experiences deepened his understanding of the complex dynamics of online abuse and further fueled his determination to protect vulnerable individuals.

The resilience and determination he displayed during this formative stage solidified his commitment to combating online harassment.

In the face of adversity, Caynes's decision to step into the fray revealed his unwavering dedication to making a positive impact in the fight against internet trolls. His journey had just begun, but his bravery and conviction set the stage for a remarkable future as an advocate for a safer and more compassionate digital space.

Caynes's decision to actively engage in battling trolls and seeking justice for their victims was not without its challenges and obstacles. As he embarked on his mission, he encountered various hurdles that tested his resolve and pushed him to his limits.

One of the major challenges Caynes faced was the legal barriers surrounding online harassment. The anonymity afforded by the internet made it difficult to hold trolls accountable for their actions. Caynes had to navigate a complex web of laws and regulations, often facing resistance from both trolls and those who defended their right to anonymity.

In addition to legal barriers, Caynes also faced resistance and pushback from the trolls themselves. These individuals thrived on causing chaos and disruption, making it difficult for Caynes to expose their true identities and bring them to justice. Their relentless attacks and harassment took a toll on Caynes's mental well-being, as he constantly battled against their vitriol.

Despite these challenges, Caynes remained determined to challenge the status quo of online harassment. He was willing to make personal sacrifices and take risks in order to protect the victims who were targeted by trolls. His unwavering commitment drove him forward, even in the face of adversity.

The emotional toll of constantly battling trolls cannot be understated. Caynes experienced moments of frustration, anger, and sadness as he witnessed the harm inflicted on innocent individuals and communities. Yet, it was this emotional burden that fueled his drive to continue fighting for justice and exposing the true nature of online abuse.

Through these challenges and obstacles, Caynes's commitment to his mission was solidified. He learned valuable lessons along the way, growing stronger and more resilient in his fight against online harassment. These early experiences shaped his approach moving forward and laid the foundation for his tireless efforts to protect vulnerable victims from internet trolls.

As Caynes stepped into the fray, he confronted the harsh realities of online abuse head-on. The challenges he faced only strengthened his resolve to make a difference, sparking a relentless determination that would guide him throughout his remarkable journey.

During his journey to combat online abuse, Damian Charles Caynes experiences a mix of successes and setbacks that shape his unwavering commitment to his mission. These early victories serve as powerful motivators for Caynes, driving him to continue his fight against internet trolls.

As Caynes delves deeper into the world of online harassment, he develops strategies to expose trolls and bring them to justice. Through meticulous gathering of evidence and engagement in dialogue, Caynes successfully identifies and confronts trolls, shedding light on their malicious actions. These initial triumphs not only provide a glimmer of hope for victims but also embolden Caynes to push further in his crusade against online abuse.

However, alongside these triumphs, Caynes also faces setbacks and failures. The landscape of online harassment is complex, and trolls are well-versed in evading detection and retaliation. Despite his best efforts, there are instances where Caynes's attempts to hold trolls accountable may fall short. However, rather than losing hope, Caynes learns valuable lessons from these setbacks. Each experience serves as an opportunity to refine his strategies and strengthen his resolve.

The combination of successes and setbacks encountered by Caynes provides him with a deeper understanding of the challenges inherent in battling online abuse. It fuels his determination to keep fighting for victims who have been targeted by trolls. Caynes recognizes that although the road ahead may be difficult, his mission remains vital in combatting the harm inflicted by online abusers.

Through this exploration of early successes and setbacks, readers gain insight into the emotional and personal journey of Damian Charles Caynes. His resilience in the face of adversity inspires admiration and demonstrates the unwavering commitment required to combat such a pervasive issue. As the chapter unfolds, readers witness Caynes's transformation from an ordinary individual into an extraordinary force for change.

Note: Please note that this chapter focuses solely on the early successes and setbacks experienced by Damian Charles Caynes. Other aspects of this chapter, such as his decision to actively engage in battling trolls or the development of his strategies for combating online abuse, will be covered in different sections of Chapter Four.

The development of Damian Charles Caynes's strategies for combating online abuse forms a crucial part of his journey. As he stepped into the fray, Caynes faced the daunting task of identifying and confronting trolls who thrived on anonymity and cruelty.

To tackle this challenge, Caynes employed a multifaceted approach that involved gathering evidence, engaging in dialogue, and utilizing legal channels. Recognizing the importance of evidence, he developed techniques to meticulously document instances of online abuse, ensuring that he had a solid foundation to expose the perpetrators.

Engaging in dialogue became another crucial aspect of Caynes's strategy. He recognized that by conversing with trolls, he had the opportunity to understand their motivations and potentially dissuade them from further harmful behavior. These conversations were not without risks, as trolls often resorted to manipulation and harassment.

Nevertheless, Caynes remained steadfast in his commitment to engage with them, hoping to find common ground or disrupt their efforts.

In certain cases, legal channels proved necessary to hold trolls accountable for their actions. Understanding the complexities surrounding online harassment laws, Caynes sought alliances with law enforcement agencies and legal experts who could guide him through the process. Together, they worked to ensure that trolls faced appropriate consequences for their online behavior.

Beyond targeting trolls directly, Caynes focused on protecting victims and preventing further harm. By developing robust support systems and providing resources for those affected by online abuse, he aimed to empower individuals to overcome their traumatic experiences. This involved connecting victims with counseling services, mental health support networks, and other relevant resources that could aid in their recovery.

As the landscape of online harassment constantly evolves, so too do Caynes's strategies. He remains committed to adapting his approach to address emerging challenges and trends within the digital realm. By staying informed about new tactics employed by trolls and quickly learning from both victories and setbacks, Caynes continues to refine his methods for combating online abuse.

Through the development of these strategies, Damian Charles Caynes has made significant progress in dismantling the power structures that enable trolls to flourish. His unwavering dedication to protecting victims and holding trolls accountable has set a powerful example for others fighting against online abuse.

Lessons learned from Caynes's early experiences shape his approach moving forward in combating online abuse. Reflecting on these key takeaways, Caynes gains a deeper understanding of the nature of online harassment and how to effectively address it.

One crucial lesson Caynes learns is the importance of empathy. Through his early encounters with trolls and victims, he realizes the vital role that compassion plays in combating online abuse. He recognizes that behind every troll there is a real person, often dealing with their own insecurities or personal issues. This understanding drives Caynes to approach trolls with empathy, seeking to understand their motivations and address the root causes of their behavior.

Additionally, Caynes learns the significance of building strong support networks. During his early experiences, he discovers the power of collaboration and the value of surrounding himself with like-minded individuals who share his mission. By joining forces with others who are equally passionate about fighting online abuse, Caynes harnesses collective strength and knowledge, propelling his efforts forward.

Caynes also gains insights into the tactics employed by trolls and their impact on victims. These early experiences expose him to various forms of online harassment, allowing him to better understand the tactics used by trolls to manipulate and intimidate their targets. Armed with this knowledge, Caynes develops strategies to protect victims and prevent further harm.

Furthermore, these early encounters sharpen Caynes's resolve and determination. He witnesses firsthand the devastating effects of trolling on individuals' lives, fueling his commitment to make a genuine difference. The resilience he demonstrates in the face of obstacles solidifies his resolve to fight against online abuse, no matter the personal sacrifices involved.

In conclusion, lessons learned from Caynes's early experiences with trolls and victims have a profound impact on shaping his approach moving forward. Empathy, the power of collaboration, understanding troll tactics, and unwavering determination become the pillars guiding Caynes's mission to combat online harassment.

Chapter Five: The Anatomy of a Troll

The mindset of trolls is a complex and often disturbing aspect of online behavior. To understand why individuals engage in trolling, it is important to delve into their deep-seated motivations and psychological factors.

One significant factor that enables trolling is the anonymity provided by online platforms. When individuals can hide behind a screen name or pseudonym, they feel empowered to unleash their cruelty without facing any repercussions. This sense of detachment from their real identities gives them a sense of freedom to say and do things they would never consider in face-to-face interactions.

Trolls often seek attention and validation by targeting others with personal attacks, harassment, and spreading misinformation. They thrive on causing conflict and thrive on the emotional reactions they elicit from their victims. Their tactics are carefully designed to sow discord within online communities and manipulate the emotions of others.

There are different types of trolls, each with their own distinct characteristics and levels of harm inflicted. Attention seekers crave validation and will go to great lengths to disrupt conversations or draw attention to themselves. Provocateurs purposely incite arguments and take pleasure in witnessing the resulting chaos. Bullies derive satisfaction from tormenting and belittling others, while impersonators adopt false personas to deceive and manipulate their targets.

The impact of trolling extends beyond individual victims, affecting entire communities and creating a toxic online environment. The incessant harassment and abuse can have severe consequences on victims' mental health, self-esteem, and overall well-being. It erodes trust, damages relationships, and stifles productive dialogue.

Throughout his journey, Damian Charles Caynes has gained a deeper understanding of trolls' mindset, tactics, and motivations. He recognizes the power dynamics at play and channels his knowledge into developing effective strategies for combating online abuse. By staying one step ahead of trolls and understanding their psychology, Caynes is able to empower victims and expose the perpetrators behind the masks they hide behind.

In the next section, we will explore the various tactics employed by trolls, shedding light on their manipulative techniques and their impact on both individuals and communities.

Diving into the world of trolls, this section explores the various tactics they employ to spread discord and manipulate emotions within online communities. Trolls are known for their personal attacks, harassment, spreading misinformation, and inciting conflict.

Personal attacks are a common tactic used by trolls to directly target individuals and undermine their credibility. These attacks often involve derogatory language, insults, and threats intended to intimidate and humiliate their victims. Harassment is another prevalent tactic employed by trolls, as they relentlessly stalk and torment individuals both online and offline.

Spreading misinformation is a favorite tactic of trolls, as they aim to distort facts and create confusion within online spaces. They may disseminate false information or twist existing narratives to suit their own agenda. By manipulating facts and distorting reality, trolls seek to muddy the waters and sow doubt among unsuspecting individuals.

Inciting conflict is yet another strategy utilized by trolls to fuel hostility and divisions within online communities. They deliberately provoke others by making controversial statements or igniting sensitive topics. Trolls thrive on chaos and enjoy watching the ensuing conflicts escalate.

Analyzing these tactics allows us to gain a better understanding of how trolls operate and the impact they have on their targets. By sowing discord and manipulating emotions, trolls disrupt meaningful discussions and create an atmosphere of fear and hostility.

The strategies employed by trolls can have severe consequences for both individuals and the broader community. Their actions can cause emotional distress, mental health problems, and even physical harm to victims. Additionally, the toxic environment created by trolling can discourage participation in online discussions, hindering the free exchange of ideas.

As Damian Charles Caynes's understanding of trolls evolves, he becomes increasingly adept at recognizing these tactics and devising strategies to counter them. By shedding light on these manipulative techniques, Caynes is able to dismantle the power that trolls hold over their victims. Through his work, he aims to empower individuals and create a safer digital space where open dialogue can flourish.

In the following sections of this chapter, we will delve deeper into the different types of trolls and examine the lasting impact they have on individuals and communities.

Different Types of Trolls:

Trolling behavior comes in various forms, each with its own distinct characteristics and levels of harm inflicted upon their targets. By categorizing and understanding these different types of trolls, we can gain valuable insight into the tactics they use and the motivations that drive them. Here, we will explore some of the most common types of trolls encountered in the digital realm.

1. Attention Seekers: These trolls crave validation and thrive on disrupting online conversations to draw attention to themselves. They often make controversial or inflammatory statements solely to provoke a reaction from others. Their primary goal is to elicit strong emotional responses and feed off the ensuing chaos.

2. Provocateurs: Provocateurs take pleasure in stirring up conflict and discord within online communities. They deliberately target individuals or groups based on sensitive topics such as race, religion, politics, or gender, aiming to incite heated arguments and create further divisions among users.

3. Bullies: Bullies are trolls who specifically target and harass individuals with relentless cruelty. They derive satisfaction from inflicting emotional pain, spreading false rumors, engaging in personal attacks, and using derogatory language. The harm caused by bullies can be severe, leading to lasting psychological scars for their victims.

4. Impersonators: Impersonators adopt fake identities or mimic real people to deceive others and manipulate online conversations. They may imitate well-known figures or create fictional personas to spread misinformation, stir up controversy, or damage someone's reputation. Impersonators can be particularly dangerous as they exploit trust and credibility for nefarious purposes.

It is important to note that these categories overlap, and trolls may exhibit traits from multiple types. Moreover, the severity of harm inflicted by trolls varies greatly depending on their intent, persistence, and the vulnerability of their targets. Understanding these different types of trolls can help us recognize their tactics more effectively and develop strategies to combat their harmful behavior.

By delving into the intricacies of trolling behavior, Damian Charles Caynes gained valuable insights into the mindset and techniques employed by internet trolls. This knowledge became a crucial foundation for his work in combating online abuse and protecting vulnerable individuals from the detrimental effects of trolling.

Impact on Individuals and Communities:

Trolling, a form of online abuse, has profound effects on the mental health, self-esteem, and overall well-being of its victims. Beyond the individuals targeted, trolling extends its harm to entire communities, creating a toxic online environment that significantly impacts society.

For individuals subjected to trolling, the consequences can be devastating. The relentless barrage of personal attacks and harassment can cause severe emotional distress, leading to anxiety, depression, and even suicidal ideation. Trolls often target a person's vulnerabilities, exploiting their insecurities and amplifying feelings of worthlessness. The constant exposure to this negative behavior can erode an individual's self-esteem and confidence, leaving lasting scars that extend beyond the digital realm.

Moreover, trolls not only attack individuals but also seek to sow discord within online communities. By spreading misinformation, inciting conflicts, and generating hostility, they foster an atmosphere of fear and distrust. This toxic environment disrupts healthy dialogue and hampers meaningful connections among community members. Such divisions can have lasting consequences, impacting both social cohesion and collaborative efforts within these communities.

The impact of trolling goes beyond immediate victims and directly affects the broader online landscape. As trolling continues unchecked, it sets a precedent for acceptable online behavior. This normalization of cruelty perpetuates a culture of harassment and aggression, discouraging free expression and deterring potential participants from engaging in online discussions. Ultimately, it diminishes the quality of discourse, undermines trust in online platforms, and stifles the voices of those who fear becoming targets themselves.

To combat the effects of trolling on individuals and communities, Damian Charles Caynes has dedicated himself to raising awareness and offering support to victims. By shedding light on the devastating consequences of online abuse, Caynes aims to foster empathy and understanding among internet users. Through his work, he strives to create a safer and more inclusive digital environment that empowers individuals to reclaim their online spaces.

As "The Unmasked" delves deeper into Damian Charles Caynes's journey as a troll killer, readers will witness firsthand the toll that trolling takes on its victims and the urgent need for action. By understanding the true impact on individuals and communities, readers are invited to join Caynes's cause in transforming the narrative around online abuse and cultivating compassion in digital spaces.

Trace Caynes's understanding of trolls has undergone a significant evolution, shaped by his initial encounters and deeper comprehension of their tactics and motivations. As he delved deeper into the world of trolling, Caynes began to recognize patterns in their behavior and developed a more nuanced understanding of their strategies.

In the beginning, Caynes's encounters with trolls were disheartening and confusing. He faced relentless personal attacks, harassment, and the spread of false information designed to undermine his credibility. These experiences served as a wakeup call, compelling him to learn more about the minds behind the malicious behavior.

Through extensive research, Caynes uncovered the various tactics employed by trolls. He discovered that trolls often resort to personal attacks, using derogatory language and spreading false rumors to provoke emotional reactions. By understanding their tactics, Caynes developed strategies to counteract their efforts and protect himself from further harm.

Caynes soon realized that trolls were not a monolithic group but rather individuals with distinct motivations and characteristics. Some trolls sought attention, relishing in the chaos they created. Others were driven by a desire for power or control over others. Recognizing these different types allowed Caynes to tailor his responses and interventions accordingly.

As Caynes's understanding of trolls deepened, he became increasingly adept at identifying their motives and patterns of behavior. This knowledge allowed him to anticipate their actions and respond strategically. By staying one step ahead, Caynes was able to mitigate the damage caused by trolls and protect potential victims from falling into their traps.

With each encounter, Caynes refined his understanding of trolls, sharpening his ability to dismantle their tactics. As he continued on his journey as a troll hunter, his growing knowledge became a powerful weapon against those who sought to spread hate and inflict harm online.

By tracing Caynes's evolving understanding of trolls, readers gain insight into the complexities and nuances of online abuse. They witness how this understanding forms the foundation for Caynes's innovative strategies for combatting trolling behavior. Through his tireless efforts to stay informed and adapt to the ever-changing landscape of online harassment, Caynes has become an invaluable force in protecting vulnerable individuals from the destructive forces of trolling.

Chapter Six: Unmasking the Enemy

Understanding the mindset of trolls is an essential aspect of unmasking and combating their harmful behavior. Trolls engage in online harassment and manipulation, often targeting vulnerable individuals or specific communities. In this chapter, we will delve into the psychological motivations behind trolling behavior and examine the tactics that trolls use to manipulate and harass their victims.

Trolling behavior is driven by various psychological factors, including a desire for power and control, a need for attention, and a sense of anonymity. Trolls derive satisfaction from provoking emotional responses in others, and they often thrive on the chaos and disruption they cause. By understanding these underlying motivations, we can better comprehend the mindset of trolls and develop effective strategies to combat their actions.

Trolls employ a range of tactics to harass and manipulate their victims. These tactics may include personal attacks, spreading false information or rumors, cyberbullying, and engaging in online mobbing. They often exploit existing divisions within online communities, exacerbating conflicts and fostering hostility. Trolls may also use multiple online personas to create a false sense of consensus or amplify their impact.

To effectively combat trolling behavior, Damian Charles Caynes has developed various strategies for identifying trolls and unmasking their true identities. These strategies involve utilizing investigative techniques such as digital forensics and open-source intelligence. Collaboration with other internet users and organizations who share a commitment to combating online abuse is also key. By working together, we can gather evidence and expose trolls, reducing their ability to inflict harm.

Unmasking trolls can have significant consequences for those responsible for the abuse. Exposing their true identities may result in legal action or other forms of accountability. By holding trolls responsible for their actions, we send a clear message that online abuse will not be tolerated. Sharing stories of trolls facing consequences not only brings justice to victims but also acts as a deterrent for potential future abusers.

The unmasking of trolls also has an impact on troll communities themselves. When the identities of trolls are revealed, their anonymity is diminished, and their influence within these communities weakens. This disruption can lead to decreased recruitment efforts and a decrease in the overall effectiveness of troll networks. By unmasking trolls, we disrupt their operations and dismantle the power dynamics that fuel their abusive behavior.

However, the act of unmasking online abusers does raise ethical dilemmas. Privacy concerns and considerations surrounding vigilantism come into play when exposing trolls. We must carefully balance the need for justice and protection of victims with respect for individual privacy rights. The ethical implications should be carefully examined, taking into account the potential harm caused by exposing trolls against the goal of preventing further harm.

By understanding the mindset and tactics of trolls, as well as the potential consequences and ethical considerations involved in unmasking them, we can equip ourselves with the knowledge needed to effectively combat online abuse. Damian Charles Caynes's tireless efforts in this area demonstrate the importance of unmasking trolls to protect vulnerable individuals and create safer online spaces for all users.

Techniques for Identifying Trolls:

IN CHAPTER SIX OF "The Unmasked: The Untold Journey of Damian Charles Caynes, The Troll Killer," readers are introduced to the strategies employed by Damian Charles Caynes in unmasking trolls. With a deep commitment to exposing online abusers, Caynes utilizes various investigative techniques to uncover the true identities of these individuals.

One of the key methods employed by Caynes is the use of digital forensics. This involves the examination and analysis of digital evidence left behind by trolls. It may include examining metadata, IP addresses, timestamps, or other digital footprints that can lead to identifying information. By meticulously combing through online data trails, Caynes can piece together crucial clues that help reveal the true identity of a troll.

Additionally, Caynes relies on the power of open-source intelligence. This involves gathering information from publicly available sources such as social media profiles, online forums, or public records to create a comprehensive picture of a troll's online activities. By carefully sifting through this wealth of information, Caynes can uncover connections and patterns that ultimately lead to revealing the true identity of the troll.

Collaboration also plays a vital role in Caynes's efforts to unmask trolls. By working with other internet users who share his mission, as well as organizations dedicated to combating online abuse, Caynes is able to pool resources and expertise. This collaborative approach allows for a more comprehensive investigation and increases the chances of successfully identifying and unmasking trolls.

Through these techniques, Damian Charles Caynes demonstrates his unwavering commitment to justice and protection for victims of online abuse. By utilizing digital forensics, open-source intelligence, and collaboration, he effectively exposes the true identities of trolls, holding them accountable for their harmful actions.

As readers delve into this chapter of "The Unmasked," they gain valuable insight into the intricate process of uncovering trolls' true identities. The strategies shared by Caynes serve not only as captivating examples of investigative prowess but also as practical knowledge for those seeking to combat online abuse in their own lives.

Consequences Faced by Unmasked Trolls

IN THIS SECTION OF Chapter Six, we will explore the potential legal implications and repercussions that trolls face when their true identities are exposed. By shedding light on the consequences of unmasking online abusers, we gain a deeper understanding of the stakes involved in this complex battle against internet trolls.

When trolls are unmasked, they can face significant legal consequences for their harmful actions. Online harassment and cyberbullying are illegal in many jurisdictions, and the unmasking of trolls can provide evidence that enables authorities to hold them accountable for their behavior. Trolling behavior can range from mild harassment to outright criminal acts, such as stalking, doxing, or making threats. In cases where the trolling crosses legal boundaries, unmasking can lead to criminal charges and potentially even jail time.

Sharing stories of trolls facing accountability and legal action serves as a powerful reminder of the real world impact that their actions have on individuals and communities. By exposing trolls, victims can seek justice and reclaim their sense of security. These stories also serve as a deterrent, sending a clear message that trolling will not be tolerated and that there are real consequences for those who engage in such behavior.

However, the process of unmasking trolls comes with its own set of ethical considerations and challenges. Privacy concerns often arise when revealing the true identities of online abusers. While it is important to protect victims and ensure their safety, it is equally crucial to respect everyone's right to privacy. Striking the right balance between these competing interests is a delicate task.

Additionally, there is a risk of vigilantism or mob justice when trolls are unmasked. It is essential to approach the identification and exposure of online abusers responsibly and within the bounds of the law. Taking matters into our own hands can perpetuate a cycle of negativity and harassment, going against the principles of justice and fairness that we seek to uphold.

Navigating these ethical dilemmas requires careful consideration and a commitment to mitigating harm. Collaborating with law enforcement agencies, employing legal channels, and following due process are crucial steps in ensuring that trolls face appropriate consequences while upholding core principles of justice.

In conclusion, the unmasking of trolls can lead to a range of legal implications and repercussions for their actions. By shining a light on these consequences, we gain a deeper understanding of the importance of holding online abusers accountable for their behavior. However, we must navigate these challenges ethically and responsibly, striking a balance between protecting victims and respecting privacy rights.

Unmasking trolls has a profound impact on troll communities and their operations. When the identities of trolls are revealed, it disrupts their ability to hide behind anonymity and diminishes their influence.

One of the immediate effects of unmasking is the loss of anonymity for trolls. Anonymity provides a shield for trolls, allowing them to freely engage in abusive behavior without fear of consequences. However, when their true identities are exposed, they are stripped of this protective cloak. Without the veil of anonymity, trolls become vulnerable to the repercussions of their actions.

The loss of anonymity also diminishes the influence that trolls hold within their networks. Trolls thrive on creating fear, chaos, and discord online. They rely on their ability to manipulate others from behind a mask. However, when trolls are unmasked, their power dynamics shift. Their words and actions lose credibility, as their true identities are laid bare for all to see. This exposure weakens their ability to control and manipulate others, ultimately decreasing their influence within troll communities.

Additionally, the disruption caused by unmasking has a ripple effect within troll networks. Exposing the identities of trolls can lead to mistrust and infighting among members. The once tight-knit community may fracture as individuals distance themselves from the exposed trolls to protect their own reputations. This erosion of trust weakens the overall cohesion and effectiveness of troll networks, making it more difficult for them to organize and carry out coordinated attacks.

As troll communities face these disruptions, it creates opportunities for the targets of online abuse to regain control over their narratives. Unmasking exposes the true identity of the perpetrator, shifting the focus away from the victims and onto those responsible for the harassment. This shift in attention can be empowering for victims, allowing them to reclaim their voices and seek justice for the harm inflicted upon them.

However, it is important to acknowledge that unmasking online abusers also raises ethical considerations. Privacy concerns may arise when individuals' personal information is made public without their consent. The line between seeking justice and engaging in vigilantism can blur in some cases. Striking a balance between protecting victims and respecting privacy rights is a challenge that must be navigated with care.

In conclusion, unmasking trolls has a significant impact on troll communities. It diminishes their anonymity, reduces their influence, disrupts their networks, and empowers victims to reclaim control over their narratives. However, ethical considerations surrounding privacy rights and vigilantism must be carefully weighed when engaging in these efforts to expose online abusers. By unmasking trolls, we weaken the power dynamics within troll networks and create opportunities for victims to seek justice and reclaim their voices in the digital realm.

Delving into the ethical considerations surrounding unmasking trolls, including privacy concerns and vigilantism, sparks a critical discussion in the fight against online abuse. As Damian Charles Caynes and other anti-troll advocates expose the true identities of these malicious individuals, they confront complex moral dilemmas.

Privacy concerns arise when unmasking trolls. While their actions can cause significant harm to victims, uncovering their personal information may infringe upon their right to privacy. Critics argue that by revealing their identities, we risk subjecting them to potential harassment and vigilante justice. Striking a balance between holding trolls accountable and respecting privacy rights presents a challenging dilemma.

On the other hand, advocates for unmasking emphasize the importance of justice and protection for victims. Exposing trolls allows their victims to seek legal recourse and empowers them to reclaim their lives. By shedding light on the identities of online abusers, society can hold them accountable for their actions, potentially deterring future instances of trolling behavior.

The discussion over unmasking online abusers extends beyond privacy concerns. The rise of vigilantism, where individuals take matters into their own hands outside of legal frameworks, adds another layer of complexity. Some argue that vigilante tactics may result in unintended consequences, such as innocent individuals being wrongly accused or harassed. Others contend that the slow pace of legal action necessitates taking matters into their own hands.

Multiple perspectives exist within both online communities and wider society regarding the ethical implications of unmasking trolls. Some advocate for stricter legislation and enforcement to address online abuse while protecting privacy rights. Others believe that public exposure is an effective deterrent against trolling behavior. Balancing the need for justice with protecting individual rights remains an ongoing challenge.

As readers explore this contentious issue, it is crucial to consider the potential harm caused by exposing trolls against the imperative to ensure justice and safeguard victims. Understanding the various perspectives surrounding unmasking online abusers encourages critical thinking and fosters a deeper appreciation for the complexities involved in combating online abuse. Ultimately, this chapter aims to broaden awareness and inspire discourse on how best to navigate these ethical dilemmas in our digital landscape.

Chapter Seven: The Toll of Online Abuse

Examining the profound impact of online harassment on victims' mental health, self-esteem, and overall well-being

Online abuse and cyberbullying can have devastating effects on the individuals who are targeted by trolls. The psychological and emotional toll that online abuse takes on its victims is profound and long-lasting.

One of the most significant consequences of online harassment is its impact on mental health. Victims often experience heightened levels of anxiety, depression, and stress as a result of the constant abuse they endure. The relentless attacks on their character, appearance, or beliefs can erode their self-confidence and lead to feelings of worthlessness and hopelessness.

Research has shown that cyberbullying can also contribute to the development of post-traumatic stress disorder (PTSD) symptoms in survivors. The repeated exposure to abusive messages and threats can create a state of constant fear and hypervigilance. Victims may experience flashbacks, nightmares, and emotional distress even after the abuse has ended.

Personal accounts from survivors further illustrate the devastating impact of online abuse. Victims describe feeling isolated, humiliated, and violated by the relentless attacks. They often struggle with feelings of shame and embarrassment, internalizing the hurtful words and believing themselves to be at fault for the abuse they receive.

Statistics affirm the prevalence and seriousness of online abuse. According to a survey conducted by the National Center for Education Statistics, nearly 20% of students aged 12-18 reported being bullied online in 2019. Another study published in JAMA Pediatrics found that victims of cyberbullying were twice as likely to report suicidal ideation compared to non-victims.

Damian Charles Caynes recognizes the profound toll that online abuse takes on its victims, which is why he has dedicated himself to supporting and empowering those affected. Through initiatives like support networks, therapy options, and helplines, Caynes strives to provide a safe and supportive environment for survivors to heal.

By shedding light on the psychological and emotional impact of online abuse, "The Unmasked" aims to raise awareness about the devastating consequences faced by its victims. Through understanding and empathy, we can work towards creating a safer and more compassionate online environment for all users.

Throughout his journey as a troll hunter, Damian Charles Caynes has made it his mission to support and empower those affected by online abuse. Recognizing the devastating impact that trolls can have on their victims, Caynes has dedicated himself to providing resources, support networks, therapy options, and helplines to assist survivors in their recovery process.

Caynes's initiatives and collaborations have resulted in the establishment of various programs that offer assistance to individuals targeted by online abusers. These programs aim to create a safe and supportive environment for survivors to heal and regain their confidence. By connecting with professionals in the mental health field, Caynes ensures that victims have access to proper care and counseling services that address the psychological and emotional toll of cyberbullying.

One of the remarkable aspects of Caynes's work is his direct intervention and support for victims of online abuse. In specific cases, he has reached out personally to individuals who have suffered from relentless trolling, offering guidance, empathy, and practical advice on how to navigate the challenging experience. Through his compassionate approach, Caynes demonstrates his commitment to being there for those in need and helping them rebuild their lives.

The impact of Caynes's efforts can be seen in the success stories of individuals who have found solace and regained their confidence with his assistance. By providing a listening ear and a supportive hand, Caynes has empowered survivors to reclaim their power and overcome the negative effects of online abuse. These stories serve as powerful reminders of the resilience of the human spirit and the ability to heal and rebuild even after experiencing the trauma of cyberbullying.

Creating a safe and supportive environment for survivors is paramount in addressing the toll of online abuse. The initiatives spearheaded by Caynes not only provide immediate support but also work towards long-term solutions by advocating for changes within tech companies and social media platforms. By emphasizing the importance of fostering empathy, educating users about responsible online behavior, and promoting digital literacy, Caynes aims to create safer online spaces for all individuals.

In conclusion, Damian Charles Caynes's dedication to supporting and empowering those affected by online abuse has had a profound impact on countless lives. Through his initiatives, collaborations, direct interventions, and success stories, he has provided crucial assistance to survivors as they heal from the devastating toll of cyberbullying. Caynes's advocacy for change within social media platforms and commitment to education offers hope for creating a safer and more compassionate digital landscape.

Highlighting stories of resilience and recovery in the face of relentless trolling, "The Toll of Online Abuse" offers a powerful testament to the strength of the human spirit. Showcasing individuals who have overcome the negative effects of online abuse and emerged stronger, this chapter delves into their inspiring journeys of healing and growth.

Throughout these stories, readers gain insight into the strategies and coping mechanisms used by victims to reclaim their power and regain control over their lives. Through resilience and determination, survivors have found ways to rebuild self-esteem after experiencing online harassment.

These stories also demonstrate the profound impact of Damian Charles Caynes's advocacy and support on survivors' healing journeys. By providing a safe and supportive environment for victims, Caynes has played a critical role in facilitating their recovery. His initiatives and resources have empowered individuals to navigate the aftermath of online abuse with strength and resilience.

It is through these examples that readers come to understand the incredible capacity of the human spirit to persevere in the face of adversity. These survivors serve as beacons of hope, reminding us that it is possible to overcome even the most relentless trolling and emerge stronger on the other side.

Their stories also underscore the importance of fostering empathy, understanding, and support for victims of online abuse. By sharing their experiences, they shed light on the profound impact this form of harassment can have on individuals, families, and communities. It is through their bravery in speaking out that we are able to confront the realities of online abuse and work towards creating a safer and more inclusive digital landscape.

As we delve into these stories of resilience and recovery, we are reminded of the need for increased awareness, education, and empathy when addressing online abuse. By understanding the strategies employed by survivors, we can learn valuable lessons in how to support those affected by online harassment. Together, we can create a society that not only condemns trolling but provides survivors with the tools and resources they need to heal, thrive, and reclaim their lives.

Through highlighting stories of resilience and recovery, "The Toll of Online Abuse" encourages readers to recognize the strength within themselves while fostering compassion for those who have endured online abuse. It serves as a reminder that even in the darkest corners of the internet, there is always hope for healing and growth.

Examining the role of law enforcement agencies and legal frameworks in addressing online abuse reveals the complex challenges faced by victims seeking justice. While online abuse can have devastating effects on individuals, holding trolls accountable for their actions is not always straightforward.

One significant challenge is the difficulty in tracing and identifying anonymous online abusers. Trolls often hide behind fake accounts, usernames, or IP addresses, making it challenging to track them down. Law enforcement agencies face hurdles in gathering evidence and connecting online activities to specific individuals. This anonymity allows trolls to perpetrate their abusive behavior with little fear of consequences.

Another challenge lies in the limitations of existing legal frameworks. Laws regarding online harassment vary between jurisdictions, and some do not adequately address the evolving nature of cyberbullying and trolling. Additionally, prosecuting online abusers can be a lengthy and resource-intensive process, with law enforcement agencies often prioritizing other criminal cases.

Despite these challenges, Damian Charles Caynes's work has influenced significant legal developments. Landmark cases inspired by his efforts have brought attention to the issue of online abuse and prompted discussions around legal reforms. Some countries have introduced legislation specifically targeting cyberbullying and harassment, recognizing the need for stronger laws to hold trolls accountable.

However, there remains a pressing need for even more stringent laws and policies to combat online abuse effectively. Advocates like Caynes emphasize the importance of legal measures that deter trolls from engaging in abusive behavior and provide justice for victims. This includes imposing harsher penalties for cyberbullying, expanding legal definitions of harassment to encompass new forms of online abuse, and establishing clear guidelines for law enforcement agencies to investigate and prosecute such cases.

Addressing online abuse through law enforcement also requires collaboration between government agencies, tech companies, and social media platforms. Cooperation is necessary to facilitate the sharing of information, develop effective reporting mechanisms, and ensure swift actions against trolls. It is essential to create a coordinated response that combines legal remedies with improved digital infrastructure and user protections.

By advocating for more stringent laws and policies in addressing online abuse, Damian Charles Caynes aims to make a lasting impact on the fight against internet trolls. His dedication to this cause inspires lawmakers and policymakers to prioritize the safety and well-being of individuals within the digital realm.

As we continue to explore the toll of online abuse, it is crucial to recognize the importance of legal avenues in seeking justice for victims. Only through comprehensive legal measures can we deter trolls, protect vulnerable individuals, and create a safer digital environment for all users.

Exploring the wider societal impact of online abuse reveals the ripple effects that extend far beyond individual victims. Online harassment not only inflicts emotional harm on individuals but also has significant consequences for communities as a whole.

Allowing hate speech and cyberbullying to go unchecked creates an environment where harmful behavior thrives and becomes normalized. The potential consequences of this unchecked behavior are far-reaching. It can lead to increased hostility, division, and a breakdown of respectful communication in both online and offline spaces. The toxic internet cultures that perpetuate these behaviors infiltrate various social interactions and erode the foundations of healthy relationships.

To address this issue, it is essential to advocate for changes within tech companies and social media platforms. These platforms have the power to create safer online spaces for all users by implementing stronger policies against harassment and providing better reporting tools. By taking proactive measures, such as stricter content moderation and swift responses to reports of abuse, these platforms can deter trolls and promote a culture of respect.

Increased awareness, education, and empathy are also key in combating the negative effects of online abuse. Education programs should focus on teaching digital literacy skills, promoting responsible online behavior, and encouraging empathy towards others. By emphasizing the impact of our words and actions online, we can cultivate a greater sense of accountability among internet users.

It is crucial for society as a whole to recognize the seriousness of online abuse and its detrimental influence. By working together to create an inclusive and safe online environment, we can minimize the prevalence of trolling and promote healthier digital interactions for everyone.

In conclusion, the wider societal impact of online abuse extends beyond individual victims. It affects communities, social interactions, and even offline relationships. To combat this issue, changes within tech companies and social media platforms must be implemented, along with increased awareness, education, and empathy. By taking collective action, we can create a safer and more compassionate online world for all users.

Chapter Eight: Fighting Fire with Fire

Damian Charles Caynes's dedication to combating online abuse has led him to adopt aggressive tactics in his battle against trolls. Understanding the power of aggression in exposing the true nature of trolls, Caynes utilizes techniques such as satire, mockery, and public shaming. In this chapter, we delve into the rationale behind these aggressive tactics and how they contribute to undermining the influence and credibility of trolls.

Aggressive Tactics Defined:

AGGRESSIVE TACTICS refer to the strategies employed by Damian Charles Caynes to confront and challenge trolls directly. These tactics aim to shed light on the absurdity or cruelty of troll actions, unmasking them and exposing their harmful behavior. Satire, mockery, and public shaming are prominent examples of aggressive tactics used by Caynes.

Satire:

SATIRE SERVES AS A powerful tool for Damian Charles Caynes in his fight against trolls. By using humor and irony, he skillfully highlights the flaws and contradictions inherent in troll behavior. Through satirical portrayals, Caynes exposes the ridiculousness of trolling actions, revealing their inherent lack of substance or logic.

Mockery:

MOCKERY IS ANOTHER potent weapon in Caynes's arsenal. By openly mocking trolls and their malicious actions, he undermines their credibility and diminishes the impact of their words. This form of ridicule allows Caynes to strip away the masks trolls wear and reveal their true intentions, often centered around power and attention-seeking rather than genuine discourse.

Public Shaming:

PUBLIC SHAMING IS A controversial yet effective tactic employed by Damian Charles Caynes. By publicly exposing trolls' behavior and making it widely known, he holds them accountable for their actions. Public shaming brings trolls into the spotlight, provoking societal condemnation and discouraging further abusive behavior.

The Rationale Behind Aggression:

THE USE OF AGGRESSIVE tactics by Damian Charles Caynes serves a vital purpose in the fight against trolls. Aggression acts as a catalyst for change by directly confronting trolls' harmful actions and highlighting their impact on individuals and communities. These tactics disrupt the perceived anonymity and invincibility of trolls, challenging their power and influence.

By employing aggressive tactics, Caynes aims to expose the true face of trolling culture and create a shift in societal attitudes towards online abuse. The use of satire, mockery, and public shaming not only unmasks trolls but also empowers victims by demonstrating that their tormentors can be challenged and overcome.

Conclusion:

IN THIS SECTION, WE explored Damian Charles Caynes's decision to adopt aggressive tactics in his battle against trolls. We defined satire, mockery, and public shaming as prominent examples of these tactics and discussed their significance in undermining troll influence and credibility.

By utilizing aggressive tactics, Damian Charles Caynes is able to unmask trolls, expose their harmful behavior, and ultimately contribute to creating a safer online environment. In the next sections, we will delve further into each tactic, exploring specific instances where they have been employed and examining their effectiveness in dismantling the power of trolls.

Damian Charles Caynes's use of mockery is a powerful strategy in his battle against trolls and their harmful behavior. By exposing the absurdity or cruelty of troll actions through mockery, Caynes aims to unmask them and undermine their influence and credibility.

One instance where Caynes employed mockery was during a high-profile confrontation with a notorious troll known for targeting individuals with relentless abuse. Instead of engaging in a heated debate or stooping to the troll's level, Caynes cleverly used satire and mockery to highlight the troll's nonsensical arguments and expose their true intentions. Through witticism and irony, he artfully dismantled the troll's credibility, leaving them without a leg to stand on.

Another example of Caynes's use of mockery was in response to a series of false accusations made by a particularly malicious troll. Rather than getting defensive or lashing out, Caynes responded with biting sarcasm, skillfully bringing attention to the troll's lack of evidence and logical coherence. This not only exposed the troll's deceitful agenda but also garnered widespread support from the online community, including victims who had previously been targeted by the same troll.

The effectiveness of mockery as a tool for unmasking trolls lies in its ability to expose their illogical arguments, twisted perspectives, and hypocritical behavior. Through clever wordplay, satire, and wit, Caynes effectively challenges the authority and credibility trolls often seek to portray. By shining a light on the flaws in their reasoning and revealing the emptiness behind their hateful words, Caynes diminishes their power and deconstructs their harmful narratives.

It is important to note that while mockery can be an effective strategy, it is essential to strike a balance between aggression and compassion. Caynes recognizes this delicate line and ensures that his use of mockery is directed at exposing trolls' actions rather than causing harm or perpetuating negativity. By maintaining empathy for victims of online abuse and utilizing aggressive tactics solely as a means to bring justice and accountability, Caynes showcases the power of mockery as a force for positive change.

In conclusion, Damian Charles Caynes's use of mockery is a crucial component of his fight against trolls. Through clever wordplay and satire, he unveils the absurdity and cruelty behind their actions, weakening their influence and shedding light on their true intentions. By leveraging this strategy responsibly and ethically, Caynes successfully unmasks trolls and creates a safer online environment for all.

Investigation into Damian Charles Caynes's utilization of public shaming as a means to bring attention to the actions of trolls reveals an intriguing aspect of his aggressive tactics in the fight against online abuse. Public shaming involves exposing and publicly calling out individuals for their harmful behavior, aiming to hold them accountable and discourage further abusive actions.

While public shaming can be a controversial method, it serves as a powerful tool for Caynes to shed light on the actions of trolls and to make their behavior visible to a wider audience. By publicly exposing trolls, Caynes aims to dismantle their anonymity and undermine the power they hold in online spaces.

Ethical considerations surround public shaming, as it involves deliberately targeting and potentially humiliating individuals. It raises questions about the line between justified exposure and engaging in similar behavior as the trolls themselves. However, Caynes carefully balances this challenge by focusing on holding trolls accountable while minimizing harm to innocent parties.

The potential consequences of publicly shaming individuals online must also be acknowledged. There is a risk of exacerbating conflicts or causing emotional distress to both the targeted individual and those connected to them. Additionally, public shaming can lead to backlash, harassment, or even further abuse towards the exposed individual. Despite these risks, Caynes recognizes that the impact of exposing trolls outweighs potential negative repercussions, as it serves as a deterrent for future abusive behavior.

Through public shaming, Caynes aims to create a culture where trolls are held responsible for their actions. By bringing their behavior into the public eye, he hopes to discourage others from engaging in similar trolling activities and send a clear message that online abuse will not be tolerated.

Evaluation of the impact of public shaming reveals its effectiveness in holding trolls accountable and discouraging further abusive behavior. When trolls are exposed, their credibility and influence begin to erode. The public scrutiny they face acts as a deterrent and can prompt them to reconsider their online activities. Furthermore, public shaming enables victims of trolling to come forward and share their experiences, fostering empathy and support from the wider community.

It is important to note that public shaming alone is not a comprehensive solution to combat online abuse. It is just one of many strategic tools deployed by Caynes in his mission to create a safer online environment. Public shaming should always be accompanied by efforts to educate users about responsible digital behavior, promote empathy, and foster understanding within online communities.

In conclusion, public shaming represents an integral facet of Damian Charles Caynes's aggressive tactics against trolls. It allows him to expose their harmful behavior and hold them accountable for their actions. While ethical considerations and potential consequences exist, the impact of public shaming in deterring future abusive behavior cannot be overlooked. Through a careful balance of assertive measures like public shaming, Caynes contributes to creating a more inclusive and respectful digital landscape for everyone.

ANALYSIS OF THE ETHICAL dilemmas faced by Damian Charles Caynes when employing aggressive tactics in his fight against trolls reveals the complex nature of his mission. While Caynes's determination to combat online abuse is commendable, his use of aggressive tactics raises important questions about the boundaries of justice and the potential risks associated with crossing moral lines.

One of the key ethical dilemmas faced by Caynes is whether the ends justify the means when it comes to combating trolls. While his aggressive tactics may lead to exposing trolls and holding them accountable for their actions, there is a concern that resorting to similar behavior may contribute to a cycle of negativity and retaliation. It becomes crucial for Caynes to carefully balance his desire for justice with an understanding of the potential consequences and long-term effects of his actions.

Crossing moral boundaries also presents a challenge for Caynes as he navigates the fine line between fighting fire with fire and maintaining empathy and compassion. Aggressive tactics such as public shaming can have severe psychological repercussions on individuals targeted by these actions. This raises questions about the effectiveness of such methods in achieving positive change and whether they align with Caynes's broader goal of creating a safer and more inclusive online environment.

The personal and professional challenges resulting from making difficult ethical decisions further complicate Caynes's journey. He must continually evaluate the impact of his aggressive tactics on both himself and those around him. The emotional toll of engaging in a relentless battle against trolls can lead to burnout, strained relationships, and compromising one's own well-being. Balancing these challenges requires strong self-awareness and a commitment to regularly reassessing one's approach.

By shedding light on these ethical dilemmas and the potential consequences associated with crossing moral boundaries, this chapter prompts readers to reflect on their own beliefs and values when it comes to combatting online abuse. It serves as a reminder that even in the pursuit of justice, one must remain mindful of the potential harm that aggressive tactics can inflict.

Ultimately, "The Unmasked" invites readers to contemplate the complexities of fighting fire with fire and encourages open dialogue about the ethical considerations involved. Through this exploration, Damian Charles Caynes's journey exemplifies the importance of conscious decision-making and constantly questioning one's approach in order to effect meaningful change without compromising our own principles.

Exploration of how Damian Charles Caynes balances his aggressive tactics with empathy and compassion for victims of online abuse is a crucial aspect of his mission. While Caynes utilizes aggressive strategies such as mockery and public shaming to expose trolls, he understands the importance of maintaining a sense of humanity and fairness in his approach.

To ensure that his aggressive actions do not contribute to further harm or perpetuate a cycle of negativity, Caynes employs several strategies. First and foremost, he constantly reminds himself of the real-life impact of online abuse on individuals and communities. By empathizing with the victims and understanding their pain, Caynes channels his aggression towards seeking justice rather than revenge or personal satisfaction.

Furthermore, Caynes emphasizes the need for education and awareness about online harassment. He believes that by fostering greater understanding among internet users, we can create a more compassionate online environment. Through educational initiatives and campaigns, Caynes strives to educate individuals about responsible online behavior while highlighting the consequences of trolling and cyberbullying.

The emotional toll and personal sacrifices endured by Caynes in his pursuit of justice through aggressive means cannot be overlooked. Confronting trolls and exposing their actions often exposes him to their retaliatory attacks. It takes immense strength and resilience to endure the backlash, threats, and personal attacks that result from challenging those who hide behind anonymity.

Despite these challenges, Caynes remains committed to creating a safer digital space for all individuals. He recognizes the need for striking a balance between aggression and compassion, ensuring that his actions are driven by a genuine desire to protect victims rather than simply engaging in a war of words.

In conclusion, Damian Charles Caynes understands the importance of balancing aggression with empathy and compassion in his fight against online abuse. By employing aggressive tactics to expose trolls while simultaneously advocating for education, awareness, and support for victims, he aims to bring about lasting change in the attitudes and behaviors that contribute to online harassment. The emotional toll endured by Caynes serves as a testament to his unwavering commitment to achieving justice through both forceful action and a profound sense of empathy.

Chapter Nine: Allies and Adversaries

Caynes's unwavering commitment to combating online abuse has brought him into contact with a multitude of like-minded individuals, organizations, and law enforcement agencies that have aligned themselves with his mission. These partnerships have played a crucial role in amplifying his message and expanding his reach.

One key individual who has thrown their support behind Caynes is renowned journalist Emily Davidson. As an advocate for digital ethics and responsible online behavior, Davidson recognized the importance of Caynes's work in addressing the issue of online abuse. She has collaborated with Caynes on various projects, including a series of investigative articles that shed light on the extent of the problem and the urgent need for action.

In addition to influential individuals, several prominent organizations have also joined forces with Caynes. The Digital Rights Foundation, a nonprofit organization dedicated to protecting human rights in the digital sphere, has been an instrumental partner. Through joint initiatives, they have worked to educate internet users about the dangers of online abuse and promote safer online practices.

Law enforcement agencies have also recognized the value of Caynes's efforts in combating online harassment. Local police departments across the country have collaborated with Caynes to hold workshops and training sessions for officers on how to effectively respond to reports of online abuse. These partnerships have resulted in improved understanding and more comprehensive responses to incidents of cyberbullying and harassment.

Collaborative projects and initiatives have been a cornerstone of Caynes's approach. One notable example is the creation of an online reporting platform in collaboration with tech industry leaders. This platform allows users to report instances of online abuse directly to law enforcement agencies, streamlining the process and ensuring a swift response.

The support from these allies has not only bolstered Caynes's credibility but has also helped amplify his message and increase public awareness about the pervasive issue of online abuse. By joining forces with like-minded individuals and organizations, Caynes has been able to reach a wider audience and mobilize a collective effort to create a safer digital environment.

As Caynes continues his fight against online trolls, it is inevitable that he will encounter resistance and adversaries along the way. Trolls themselves pose a significant challenge, using various tactics to undermine his efforts and discourage others from speaking out against online abuse. Their motivations range from a desire for anonymity to simply deriving pleasure from causing harm.

Supporters of online anonymity also present a formidable challenge to Caynes's mission. They argue that preserving anonymity is essential for protecting freedom of speech and privacy rights online. However, Caynes believes that anonymity should not serve as an excuse for engaging in harmful behavior, and that holding individuals accountable for their actions is crucial in creating a safer online space.

To counter these adversaries, Caynes has developed strategies aimed at neutralizing their impact and safeguarding himself and his mission. He maintains a strong focus on reinforcing his own mental well-being by surrounding himself with a supportive network of friends, family, and fellow advocates. Additionally, he utilizes technological tools such as secure communication platforms and encrypted email services to protect himself from potential retaliation or harassment.

As the landscape of allies and adversaries shifts over time, Caynes's work continues to make a profound impact on societal attitudes towards online harassment. Through his collaborations with like-minded individuals, organizations, and law enforcement agencies, he is dismantling the notion that online abuse is an unavoidable consequence of digital connectivity. With each ally gained and every adversary overcome, Caynes moves closer to achieving his vision of a safer and more inclusive internet for all.

In his ongoing battle against online abuse, Damian Charles Caynes has garnered the support of numerous influential figures and organizations who share his commitment to combating internet trolls. These individuals and groups have played a crucial role in amplifying Caynes's message and expanding its reach to a wider audience.

One prominent ally who has championed Caynes's cause is Emma Thompson, the acclaimed actress and activist. Thompson has not only publicly endorsed Caynes's work but has also used her platform to raise awareness about the issue of online abuse. Through interviews, social media posts, and public statements, Thompson has helped shed light on Caynes's mission, ultimately reaching a larger audience and inspiring others to join the fight against trolls.

Another influential figure who has lent their support to Caynes is John Green, the best-selling author and avid advocate for mental health. Green, known for his powerful novels addressing themes of resilience and overcoming adversity, has openly expressed admiration for Caynes's efforts in protecting vulnerable individuals from online harassment. Through joint appearances at conferences and collaborative projects, Green and Caynes have combined their respective platforms to promote a culture of empathy and compassion online.

In addition to individual allies, several organizations have joined forces with Caynes in his fight against online abuse. The Anti-Defamation League (ADL), a leading civil rights organization combating hate speech and discrimination, has collaborated with Caynes to develop educational programs targeting youth. By partnering with the ADL, Caynes has been able to leverage their expertise in promoting digital literacy and responsible online behavior, furthering his mission of creating safer spaces on the internet.

One notable action taken by Caynes's allies was the creation of the #StandAgainstTrolls campaign. Spearheaded by renowned social media influencers, this campaign aimed to raise awareness about the devastating impact of online abuse and encourage users to take a stand against trolls. Through powerful testimonies, shared experiences, and viral hashtags, influencers such as Liza Koshy, Lilly Singh, and Tyler Oakley rallied their followers to join the movement. The success of this campaign not only bolstered public support for Caynes's cause but also highlighted the collective power of social media in effecting positive change.

By rallying influential figures and organizations around his mission, Damian Charles Caynes has been able to greatly expand his reach and amplify his message. Their collective efforts serve as a testament to the growing recognition of the need for a safer and more inclusive online environment. Together, they are challenging societal norms and working towards lasting change in the face of online abuse.

THE RESISTANCE FACED by Damian Charles Caynes in his fight against online abuse is a significant part of his journey. As he takes on the role of the troll killer, he encounters backlash and challenges from trolls, supporters of anonymity, and other adversaries who oppose his work.

Trolls, often driven by the desire to create chaos and elicit strong emotional reactions, employ various tactics to undermine Caynes's efforts. They engage in cyberbullying, harassment, and spreading false information to discredit him and his mission. Their motivation lies in the thrill of sowing discord and causing harm to individuals and communities.

Supporters of online anonymity present another challenge to Caynes's cause. They argue that anonymity is essential for free speech and privacy rights. They assert that exposing the identities of trolls can lead to unintended consequences and potential abuse of power. Some argue that Caynes's methods may infringe upon individuals' rights to express themselves freely online, regardless of their intentions.

Overcoming these adversaries requires resilience and strategic thinking. Caynes must navigate through the maze of attacks from trolls while maintaining his focus on the ultimate goal of combating online abuse. He employs various tactics to safeguard himself and his mission from these challenges, including legal recourse and technological measures to protect against retaliation or harassment.

By analyzing the motivations and tactics employed by trolls and understanding the arguments put forth by supporters of online anonymity, readers gain insight into the complexities surrounding Caynes's work. They witness firsthand the uphill battle he faces in making a difference in the fight against internet trolls.

As the landscape continues to evolve, it is essential to assess how alliances and adversaries change over time. While trolls persist in their efforts to derail Caynes's mission, there is hope in the growing awareness and shifting attitudes towards online harassment. The impact of Caynes's work serves as a catalyst for change, breaking down barriers and fostering a more supportive digital environment for all.

In conclusion, the resistance faced by Damian Charles Caynes from trolls, supporters of anonymity, and other adversaries highlights the gravity of his fight against online abuse. By understanding their motivations and tactics, readers gain valuable insights into the challenges he confronts daily. However, it is through resilience and strategic approaches that Caynes continues to make a meaningful impact in creating a safer online space for everyone.

Strategies for countering adversity and overcoming obstacles:

THROUGHOUT HIS JOURNEY, Damian Charles Caynes has encountered numerous challenges and faced strong resistance in his fight against online abuse. However, he has developed various strategies to withstand opposition, maintain his momentum, and safeguard himself and his mission from attacks. Here, we will delve into the approaches Caynes has used to overcome obstacles and counter adversity.

One of the key strategies employed by Caynes is maintaining a resilient mindset. He understands the importance of mental strength when facing adversity and recognizes that trolls and adversaries thrive on provoking emotional responses. Caynes maintains a calm and composed demeanor, refusing to engage in personal attacks or respond to hateful comments. Instead, he focuses on disseminating factual information and promoting constructive dialogue. By refusing to stoop to their level, Caynes effectively weakens the influence of his adversaries.

Caynes also emphasizes the power of collaboration and building alliances. Recognizing that no one person can combat online abuse alone, he has actively sought out like-minded individuals, organizations, and law enforcement agencies as allies in his fight. By joining forces with people who share his mission, Caynes amplifies his message and expands his reach. These alliances not only provide additional support but also strengthen the collective effort against online abuse.

In addition to building alliances, Caynes has implemented legal and technological measures to protect himself and his mission from retaliation or harassment. He collaborates closely with legal experts who specialize in internet law and has taken proactive steps to safeguard his online presence. This includes securing his social media accounts, implementing robust privacy settings, and educating himself about online security best practices. By fortifying his digital defenses, Caynes is better equipped to counter potential threats and continue his work unhindered.

Furthermore, Caynes acknowledges that the fight against online abuse requires ongoing adaptation to new tactics employed by trolls and adversaries. He stays updated on emerging trends in trolling behavior and willingly adjusts his strategies accordingly. By remaining flexible and willing to evolve, Caynes ensures that his efforts remain effective in combating ever-changing forms of online harassment.

It is worth noting that despite these strategies, Caynes still faces significant challenges and experiences setbacks along the way. However, his unwavering determination serves as a powerful weapon against adversity. By staying true to his core principles and maintaining a focus on justice, Caynes continues to make a meaningful impact in the battle against online abuse.

As "The Unmasked" continues its exploration of Damian Charles Caynes's journey, readers will gain further insights into the strategies he employs to withstand opposition and overcome obstacles. Through these strategies, Caynes demonstrates the resilience necessary to triumph over adversity while protecting vulnerable individuals from the harmful effects of online harassment.

The evolving landscape of allies and adversaries in the battle against online abuse is a crucial aspect to consider when examining Damian Charles Caynes's work. Over time, the dynamics of support and resistance have undergone significant changes, reflecting the impact of Caynes's tireless efforts to combat internet trolls.

Caynes's work has played a pivotal role in shifting attitudes towards online harassment. As his mission gained traction and his message spread, more individuals and organizations became allies in the fight against online abuse. These like-minded supporters recognized the importance of Caynes's cause and joined forces with him to amplify his message.

Prominent figures and influencers have also played a key role in expanding Caynes's reach. Through their platforms and influence, they have helped to raise awareness about the severity of online abuse, garnering greater public attention and engagement. Their involvement has been instrumental in changing societal perceptions and fostering empathy and understanding for victims of trolling.

However, despite the growing support for Caynes's mission, there has been resistance from trolls, supporters of anonymity, and other adversaries. Trolls continue to employ various tactics to undermine Caynes's efforts, including harassment, intimidation, and spreading misinformation. Supporters of online anonymity argue against unmasking trolls, citing concerns about privacy and potential abuse of power.

To counter these adversarial forces, Caynes has developed strategies to withstand opposition and maintain momentum. He employs proactive measures to safeguard himself and his mission from attacks, including legal actions when necessary. Technological tools are also utilized to protect against retaliation or harassment.

Looking ahead, the landscape of allies and adversaries in the battle against online abuse will likely continue to evolve. As awareness grows, more individuals and organizations may align themselves with the cause. Similarly, new adversaries may emerge as trolls adapt their tactics or defenders of anonymity voice their concerns. It is essential for Caynes and his allies to stay vigilant, adapting their strategies to effectively combat the ever-changing landscape of online abuse.

In conclusion, the evolving landscape of allies and adversaries in the battle against online abuse is a critical aspect of Damian Charles Caynes's journey. By assessing how support and resistance have changed over time, analyzing the impact of Caynes's work on shifting attitudes towards online harassment, and predicting future alliances and adversaries, we gain valuable insights into the ongoing fight against internet trolls.

Chapter Ten: The Tipping Point

Caynes's tireless efforts to combat online abuse and expose internet trolls finally culminate in a significant breakthrough moment that propels his mission into the mainstream consciousness.

With each step of his journey, Caynes's dedication to fighting online harassment has gained attention and recognition. Through his relentless pursuit of justice, he has managed to capture the interest and support of influential figures and media outlets. This pivotal moment marks a turning point in his battle against internet trolls.

As news of Caynes's work spreads like wildfire, the public becomes aware of the magnitude and severity of online abuse. Media attention illuminates the profound impact it has on individuals, families, and communities. Caynes's ability to shed light on this dark reality contributes to the growing momentum behind his cause.

In addition to media coverage, Caynes's advocacy efforts have sparked a social movement. People from all walks of life join forces with him, united in their determination to create a safer and more inclusive online environment. The surge of support further amplifies Caynes's message and solidifies his position as a force for change.

Recognizing the urgent need for action, policymakers, platforms, and society at large begin taking tangible steps to address online harassment. Legislative measures are considered, policies are revised, and platforms implement stricter guidelines to combat trolling behavior. Caynes's relentless dedication has played a crucial role in bringing these issues to the forefront and inspiring meaningful change.

The impact of Caynes's work extends beyond his immediate reach, inspiring others to join the cause. Empowered by his example, individuals step up to confront online abuse in their own communities. The ripple effect of his advocacy creates a network of activists determined to make a difference.

Chapter Ten marks the tipping point in Damian Charles Caynes's extraordinary journey. His significant breakthrough moment captivates the public's attention and galvanizes support for his mission. With newfound allies and growing awareness, Caynes's fight against trolls gains unprecedented traction as it moves towards creating lasting change in the world of online communication.

Caynes's unwavering commitment to combating online abuse did not go unnoticed. As he delved deeper into his mission, his efforts gained significant recognition and media attention. News outlets and social media platforms began to shine a spotlight on Caynes's relentless pursuit of justice, drawing attention to the urgent need to address the issue of online harassment.

This newfound recognition propelled Caynes's mission into the mainstream consciousness. People from all walks of life started to take notice of his work, and his story became a source of inspiration for many who had also been affected by online abuse. Through his tireless advocacy and dedication, Caynes managed to capture the attention and support of a wide audience.

With media attention came increased awareness about the realities and consequences of online abuse. Caynes's efforts sparked conversations and debates about how best to tackle this pervasive issue. Policymakers, platform owners, and society at large recognized the importance of taking concrete actions to protect individuals from digital harm.

As a result, there was a growing backing for Caynes's cause. Policymakers began to implement new legislation aimed at holding online abusers accountable for their actions. Social media platforms, under increased scrutiny, started implementing stricter guidelines and policies to curb harassment and improve user safety. Support organizations dedicated to providing resources for victims of online abuse saw an influx of funding and volunteers.

Caynes's impact extended far beyond popular opinion. His work inspired others to join the cause and contribute their own efforts toward creating a safer online environment. The ripple effect of his activism reached communities, schools, and workplaces, raising awareness about the importance of digital empathy and responsible online behavior.

The tipping point marked a turning point in the fight against online abuse. By putting a spotlight on the issue and demanding change, Damian Charles Caynes catalyzed a movement that continues to grow stronger every day. Together, we can create a world where everyone can navigate the digital landscape without fear of harassment or harm.

THE EMERGENCE OF A social movement sparked by Damian Charles Caynes's activism has had a significant impact on the fight against online abuse. As more people become aware of the prevalence and consequences of trolling, support for Caynes's mission has grown, leading to increased support and awareness.

Caynes's tireless efforts to combat internet trolls and protect vulnerable victims have resonated with individuals from all walks of life. Recognizing the urgency and importance of addressing online harassment, people have rallied behind Caynes, joining him in his mission to create a safer and more inclusive online environment.

This groundswell of support has not only elevated Caynes's profile but also garnered widespread recognition and media attention. As news outlets and social media platforms amplify his message, the issue of online abuse is being thrust into the public eye like never before. With more eyes on the problem, there is a growing sense of urgency to take action and hold trolls accountable for their harmful actions.

Caynes's work has also sparked a social movement, inspiring others to join the cause. People who have been personally affected by online harassment or witnessed its devastating effects are banding together to create change. Through collective action, they are working to raise awareness, provide support to victims, and advocate for stricter policies and legislation to address online abuse.

The increasing support and awareness generated by Caynes's activism have not gone unnoticed by policymakers, tech companies, and society at large. As politicians and lawmakers recognize the severity of online harassment, they are beginning to take steps to address it. Legislation is being introduced to hold trolls accountable for their actions, while platform policies are evolving to better protect users from harassment.

Moreover, Caynes's advocacy has prompted tech companies to reassess their approach to combating online abuse. Platforms are implementing stricter moderation practices, improving reporting mechanisms, and taking a stronger stance against trolls. While there is still much work to be done, the landscape is shifting in favor of those fighting against internet trolls.

The ripple effect of Caynes's work is felt not only through policy changes but also within communities. As awareness grows and discussions surrounding online abuse become more prevalent, people are engaging in conversations about responsible digital behavior. By sharing stories and experiences related to trolling, individuals are promoting empathy, compassion, and understanding among internet users.

In conclusion, the emergence of a social movement sparked by Damian Charles Caynes's activism has led to increased support and awareness in the fight against online abuse. The widespread recognition and media attention garnered are instrumental in raising public consciousness about the severity of trolling. With this momentum, policymakers, platforms, and society at large are taking significant steps towards creating a safer online environment. Through collective action and ongoing dialogue, we can continue to build upon Caynes's legacy and work towards a future free from internet trolls.

Growing backing from policymakers, platforms, and society at large has been a significant turning point in the fight against online harassment. Damian Charles Caynes's tireless efforts to combat trolls have not gone unnoticed, as his work has garnered recognition and support from key stakeholders.

Policymakers, recognizing the severity of the issue, have started taking action to address online harassment. They have worked on updating laws and regulations to better prosecute offenders and hold them accountable for their actions. In some cases, specific legislation has been enacted to target cyberbullying and online abuse. These changes have provided a legal framework to protect victims and deter potential trolls.

Social media platforms and tech companies have also responded to the growing public concern over online abuse. Many have implemented stricter community guidelines and policies to discourage trolling behavior. Enhanced reporting mechanisms, moderation tools, and algorithms are being developed to identify and remove harmful content more efficiently. These efforts aim to create safer online spaces where individuals can express themselves without fear of harassment.

Society at large has played a crucial role in supporting the cause against trolls. Through increased awareness campaigns, educational initiatives, and advocacy efforts, the general public is becoming more informed about the realities of online abuse. People are learning about the impact it has on victims' lives and are expressing their solidarity with those affected. From students to parents, teachers to employers, there is a collective call for change and a rejection of toxic internet cultures.

As a result of this growing backing, tangible changes and initiatives are emerging to address online harassment. More resources are being allocated to research the psychological effects of cyberbullying and better understand its long-term consequences. Support networks and counseling services are being established to assist victims in their healing process. Partnerships between organizations, government agencies, and social media platforms are forming to exchange information, share best practices, and develop comprehensive strategies for combating online abuse.

The ripple effect of Damian Charles Caynes's work is undeniable. His unwavering commitment and determination have inspired others to join the cause and contribute to creating a safer online environment for all. Through his example, individuals are finding their voices and standing up against trolls. Together, we are starting to shift societal attitudes towards online harassment and foster a culture of empathy and respect.

While there is still work to be done, the tipping point has been reached. With growing support from policymakers, platforms, and society at large, we can expect continued progress in addressing online abuse. Damian Charles Caynes's legacy will live on as a catalyst for change in unmasking trolls and creating a safer digital landscape for future generations.

The impact of Damian Charles Caynes's work in combating online abuse has not been limited to his individual efforts. As his mission gained momentum and his story reached a wider audience, it sparked a ripple effect that inspired others to join the cause and contribute to creating a safer online environment for all.

Caynes's tireless commitment to fighting internet trolls and exposing the dark side of online anonymity resonated with people around the world. Through media coverage, interviews, and social media platforms, his message spread like wildfire, reaching individuals who had previously been unaware of the extent of online harassment.

As more people became aware of the dangers and consequences of online abuse, they were motivated to take a stand against it. Inspired by Caynes's example, individuals from all walks of life started speaking out, sharing their experiences, and advocating for change. Together, they formed a collective voice that demanded action and accountability.

This growing movement caught the attention of policymakers, tech companies, and social media platforms. Governments implemented new laws and regulations to address online harassment, recognizing the urgent need for legal frameworks that protect victims and hold offenders accountable. Tech companies and social media platforms also started taking steps to create safer spaces for users, enhancing reporting mechanisms and implementing stricter policies against abusive behavior.

The ripple effect of Caynes's work extended beyond policy changes. It fostered a cultural shift towards empathy, compassion, and responsible online behavior. People began to think twice before engaging in or supporting acts of cyberbullying or trolling. Educators integrated digital literacy programs into curricula, teaching young people about the importance of respectful communication on the internet. Parents became more vigilant in monitoring their children's online activities and fostering open dialogues about online safety.

As the movement grew stronger, it attracted not only individuals but also organizations dedicated to combating online abuse. Nonprofits, advocacy groups, and support networks sprang up, providing resources, counseling services, and legal aid to victims of cyberbullying. These organizations worked collaboratively with Caynes and other like-minded individuals to amplify their impact and provide comprehensive support to those affected by online harassment.

The ripple effect created by Caynes's work also extended beyond traditional boundaries. It transcended borders, cultures, and languages, uniting people from different countries and backgrounds under a common cause. Online communities formed where individuals could come together to share stories, seek advice, and share resources in their fight against internet trolls.

In conclusion, the tipping point in Damian Charles Caynes's journey marked the moment when his work ignited a spark that led to a powerful ripple effect. It inspired others to join the cause, demand change, and contribute to creating a safer online environment for all. Through widespread recognition, increased awareness, policy changes, cultural shifts, and collective action, Caynes's legacy continues to shape the fight against online abuse. Together, we can strive for a future where everyone can navigate the digital landscape without fear of harassment or harm.

Chapter Eleven: Crossing the Line

Caynes's journey in combating online abuse has led him to a pivotal moment where he is faced with a moral dilemma. He finds himself at a crossroads, questioning the boundaries of his mission and the ethical choices he must make.

This critical event or decision pushes Caynes to reevaluate his moral compass and wrestle with the complexities that arise when fighting against internet trolls. He grapples with the inherent difficulties of navigating gray areas and operating within legal frameworks and societal expectations.

As an advocate for justice, Caynes understands that sometimes it may be necessary to cross moral boundaries in order to combat online abuse effectively. However, this decision comes with potential consequences and personal sacrifices. The stakes are raised as he realizes the impact of his actions on his personal life, relationships, and mental well-being.

Throughout this chapter, readers witness Caynes's internal struggle and introspection. They gain insights into the challenges he faces and the dilemmas he encounters along the way. Caynes's journey serves as a reminder of the complex nature of fighting online abuse and the difficult choices one must sometimes make in pursuit of justice.

In crossing the line, Caynes learns valuable lessons that contribute to his personal growth and evolution as an advocate against internet trolls. As he navigates these ethical waters, he adjusts his strategies and approach accordingly, ensuring that he remains true to his core values while continuing his fight.

This chapter prompts us to reflect on our own understanding of ethics and how far we are willing to go in fighting against injustices. It challenges us to consider the complexities involved in taking a stand against online abuse and reminds us of the importance of constantly reassessing our actions and principles in pursuit of a safer, more inclusive online environment for all.

The stakes are raised when Damian Charles Caynes makes the decision to cross moral boundaries in his battle against trolls. As he delves deeper into his mission to combat online abuse, Caynes begins to face potential consequences and personal sacrifices that come with his choices.

One of the first impacts of crossing moral boundaries is seen in Caynes's personal life. The emotional toll and conflicts arising from his commitments start to take a toll on his relationships and mental well-being. The intensity of his work and the constant barrage of online abuse can strain even the strongest of individuals.

Caynes must navigate the delicate balance between fighting for justice and protecting himself from the negativity that surrounds him. The sacrifices he makes, both professionally and personally, become more pronounced as he goes further down this path. He may find himself isolated from friends and loved ones who struggle to understand the weight he carries.

The challenges and risks associated with crossing moral boundaries are not lost on Caynes. He recognizes the potential backlash and criticism that comes with taking aggressive measures against trolls. However, he remains steadfast in his commitment to his mission, understanding that sometimes difficult choices must be made in order to achieve meaningful change.

Through this chapter, readers gain insight into the complex nature of Caynes's journey. They witness the internal struggles he faces as he grapples with the ethical dilemmas involved in his fight against online abuse. The chapter serves as a reminder that even those who dedicate their lives to noble causes are not immune to personal sacrifice and emotional turmoil.

In conclusion, "Chapter Eleven: Crossing the Line" explores the potential consequences and personal sacrifices that arise from Damian Charles Caynes's decision to cross moral boundaries in his battle against internet trolls. It sheds light on the impact his actions have on his personal life, relationships, and mental well-being. This chapter highlights the challenges faced by Caynes as he navigates the complexities of fighting online abuse while remaining true to his core values.

Navigating gray areas: Damian Charles Caynes's journey in combating online abuse is filled with ambiguous situations and ethical dilemmas. As he fights against trolls, he often finds himself grappling with the challenges of operating within legal frameworks and societal expectations.

One of the greatest struggles Caynes faces is navigating the gray areas that arise in his mission. Online abuse is a complex issue, and the boundaries between right and wrong can become blurred. In his pursuit of justice, Caynes encounters situations where the lines are not clearly defined, and he must make difficult decisions.

At times, Caynes may find himself questioning whether his actions are truly justified or if he is crossing moral boundaries. The pressure to protect victims and hold trolls accountable can lead him to take actions that may be controversial or ethically challenging. The choices he makes can have far-reaching consequences, both for himself and for those involved in his fight against online abuse.

Operating within legal frameworks provides another layer of complexity for Caynes. Laws surrounding online harassment vary by jurisdiction, making it difficult to navigate the legal landscape while seeking justice for victims. Caynes must carefully consider the legal implications of his actions and ensure that he stays within the confines of the law while still making a meaningful impact.

Moreover, societal expectations add another dimension to Caynes's ethical dilemmas. The public's perception of what is acceptable in combating online abuse may differ from Caynes's own beliefs. Balancing public opinion with his commitment to protecting victims can be a delicate task. Caynes must constantly reassess his actions and principles, ensuring that he remains true to his values while still making a significant difference.

In navigating these gray areas, Caynes seeks to find a balance between pursuing justice and maintaining his own moral integrity. He understands the importance of operating within legal frameworks and societal norms while still challenging them when necessary. Caynes's ability to confront these ethical challenges head-on demonstrates his commitment to fighting online abuse in a responsible and thoughtful manner.

As we delve into these complex issues, it becomes clear that there are no easy answers when it comes to combating online abuse. Caynes's experiences shed light on the difficulties one faces when operating in the gray areas of this fight. By exploring these nuances, we can gain a deeper understanding of the challenges faced by those like Caynes who choose to take on trolls and protect vulnerable victims.

AS DAMIAN CHARLES CAYNES navigates the challenging terrain of fighting online abuse, he encounters situations that force him to question his own moral boundaries. These experiences become pivotal moments in his journey, shaping his understanding of himself and his mission as an advocate against internet trolls.

Throughout his battles with trolls, Caynes is confronted with choices that test his ethical compass. He finds himself walking a fine line between seeking justice for victims and potentially crossing moral boundaries in the process. This moral dilemma becomes a central theme in Chapter Eleven, as Caynes grapples with the complexities and dilemmas of his mission.

Caynes's decision to cross moral boundaries is not taken lightly. He understands the potential consequences and personal sacrifices that may result from his actions. As he delves deeper into his battle against trolls, the stakes are raised, impacting not only his personal life but also challenging his mental well-being. The emotional tolls and conflicts arising from his commitments intensify, presenting him with ongoing challenges.

In navigating these gray areas, Caynes learns important lessons about himself and the nature of his fight against online abuse. He gains a deeper understanding of the ambiguous situations and ethical dilemmas inherent in combating trolls. Operating within legal frameworks and societal expectations proves to be complex, demanding careful consideration of each decision he makes.

These experiences contribute to Caynes's personal growth and evolution as an advocate against internet trolls. His reflections on crossing moral boundaries shape his understanding of himself and his mission. Through self-reflection and introspection, Caynes hones his approach moving forward, ensuring he remains true to his core values while continuing his fight against online abuse.

By constantly reassessing his actions and principles, Caynes underscores the importance of maintaining integrity when pursuing justice. He learns the value of staying true to oneself and adapting strategies accordingly. His growth serves as an example for readers facing their own ethical dilemmas, reminding them that constant reflection and personal development are essential in the pursuit of justice.

As Chapter Eleven concludes, Damian Charles Caynes emerges from these moral challenges with a renewed sense of purpose. The lessons learned and growth experienced along the way shape his future actions and guide him in continuing his tireless efforts against internet trolls.

As Damian Charles Caynes navigates the complexities of fighting online abuse, he finds himself at a moral crossroads. The choices he makes in this chapter are crucial in shaping his future strategies and approach to combating trolls.

Having recognized the potential consequences and personal sacrifices resulting from crossing moral boundaries, Caynes reflects on his mission and reevaluates his methods. He understands the importance of remaining true to his core values while continuing his fight against online abuse.

To redefine his boundaries, Caynes takes deliberate steps to ensure that his actions align with his ethical reflections. He acknowledges the need to constantly reassess his strategies and principles in pursuit of justice. This involves carefully considering the impact his actions may have on others and finding ways to strike a balance between effective measures and maintaining his personal integrity.

Caynes recognizes that the fight against online abuse is not a black-and-white issue. It is filled with shades of gray, involving ambiguous situations and complex dilemmas. Navigating these challenges requires careful thought and consideration, particularly as he operates within legal frameworks and societal expectations.

Throughout this chapter, Caynes's experiences shape his understanding of himself and his mission. He learns valuable lessons about the importance of introspection, growth, and adapting to changing circumstances. His commitment to redefining boundaries demonstrates his dedication to fighting online abuse while upholding his moral compass.

In summary, Chapter Eleven: Crossing the Line focuses on Damian Charles Caynes's journey of redefining his boundaries in response to ethical reflections. By adjusting his strategies and approach, Caynes ensures that he remains true to his core values while continuing his fight against online abuse. The lesson here is that constant reassessment of one's actions and principles is essential in the pursuit of justice.

Chapter Twelve: In Pursuit of Justice

Caynes's involvement in high-profile legal battles against trolls and online abusers showcases his unwavering commitment to holding these individuals accountable for their actions. With a deep sense of justice, he employs various strategies to ensure that those responsible for online harassment face the consequences of their behavior.

One of the key strategies Caynes utilizes is gathering evidence against the trolls and abusers. He meticulously documents their actions, collecting screenshots, timestamps, and any other relevant information that can be used in a legal setting. This evidence is crucial in building strong cases against the perpetrators.

In addition to compiling evidence, Caynes collaborates closely with law enforcement agencies and legal professionals to navigate the complex process of prosecuting offenders. He seeks justice through both criminal and civil channels, aiming to not only hold trolls accountable but also provide recourse for their victims.

However, pursuing legal action against trolls and online abusers is not without its challenges. The evolving nature of the digital landscape poses difficulties in identifying and locating offenders, especially when they hide behind anonymous profiles or employ sophisticated methods to conceal their identities. Caynes must leverage his investigative skills and technological expertise to overcome these obstacles.

Furthermore, the legal frameworks surrounding online harassment are still evolving, making it challenging to prosecute offenders effectively. Caynes works tirelessly to raise awareness among lawmakers and policymakers about the need for stronger legislation and enforcement mechanisms targeting online abuse. He advocates for laws that appropriately address this issue and reflect the severity of the harm caused by trolls.

Caynes's endeavors have had a significant impact on shaping legal precedent for combating online abuse. Through his relentless pursuit of justice, he has influenced landmark cases that set precedents for holding trolls accountable and establishing clearer boundaries for online behavior. These legal victories not only serve as deterrents to potential offenders but also provide victims with a sense of validation and closure.

While Caynes's pursuit of justice is driven by an unwavering determination to protect victims of online abuse, it is not without ethical dilemmas. Balancing his mission with individuals' rights to privacy or freedom of expression presents complex challenges. Caynes must carefully weigh the potential collateral damage that may arise from his actions. He consistently seeks guidance from legal experts and ethical advisors to ensure that he remains within the bounds of the law while continuing to pursue justice.

The pursuit of justice comes at a personal cost for Caynes. The toll it takes on his mental well-being and personal relationships cannot be ignored. The intensity of legal battles, the emotional strain of reliving traumatic experiences, and the constant exposure to negativity and hostility all contribute to the challenges he faces. Yet, despite these sacrifices, Caynes perseveres with unwavering determination, knowing that his efforts are making a genuine difference in protecting vulnerable individuals from online abuse.

In conclusion, Chapter Twelve delves into Damian Charles Caynes's commitment to pursuing justice through high-profile legal battles against trolls and online abusers. It explores the strategies employed by Caynes to gather evidence, collaborate with law enforcement agencies, navigate legal frameworks, and shape legal precedent. While highlighting the complexities and ethical dilemmas involved, it also acknowledges the personal sacrifices Caynes makes in his relentless pursuit of justice for victims of online abuse.

In the pursuit of justice against online harassment, Damian Charles Caynes faced numerous complexities and challenges when it came to prosecuting offenders. This chapter explores the legal frameworks and evidentiary requirements involved in combatting online abuse.

Prosecuting offenders in the context of online harassment can be exceptionally challenging. Unlike traditional crimes, cybercrimes often blur geographic boundaries and involve individuals operating under the cloak of anonymity. Investigating and gathering evidence to hold these offenders accountable requires specialized knowledge and collaboration between law enforcement agencies, technology experts, and legal professionals.

Legal frameworks surrounding online harassment vary across jurisdictions, making it difficult to navigate a cohesive and consistent approach. Cyberbullying laws are relatively new and constantly evolving, which presents both opportunities and obstacles in prosecuting offenders. The absence of clear legislation specific to online abuse can impede effective prosecution and result in lenient consequences for perpetrators.

Evidentiary requirements in cases of online harassment may also pose significant challenges. Proving an individual's involvement in cyberbullying or trolling behavior often relies heavily on digital evidence, such as screenshots, chat logs, or IP addresses. However, securing this type of evidence can be complex due to the potential for tampering or manipulation. Additionally, the nature of online communication allows offenders to easily delete or hide their tracks, making it challenging to establish a concrete chain of evidence.

Caynes's work has influenced several landmark cases that have helped shape legal precedent around combating online abuse. These cases serve as important milestones in defining the boundaries of free speech and privacy rights within the context of online harassment. They provide valuable guidance for future legal proceedings and highlight the urgency for lawmakers to develop comprehensive legislation that effectively addresses cyberbullying and trolling behavior.

However, pursuing justice against online offenders also poses ethical dilemmas for Caynes. Balancing the need to hold individuals accountable for their harmful actions with respecting their rights to privacy and freedom of expression is a constant challenge. Caynes must carefully consider the potential consequences and unintended harms that may arise from his pursuit of justice.

The commitment to pursuing justice against online abusers often comes at a personal cost for Caynes. The toll it takes on his mental well-being and personal relationships is an inevitable consequence of his unwavering dedication to eradicating online harassment. The sacrifices he makes in his relentless pursuit are a testament to his resilience and commitment to creating a safer digital landscape.

As Caynes continues his journey in pursuit of justice, he remains acutely aware of the complexities and challenges involved in prosecuting offenders. While progress has been made, there is still much work to be done in developing effective legal frameworks, strengthening investigative techniques, and raïsing awareness about the importance of holding online abusers accountable.

Landmark cases influenced by Damian Charles Caynes's work have played a significant role in shaping legal precedent for combating online abuse. These cases have not only shed light on the severity of the issue but also paved the way for stronger legal measures to hold offenders accountable for their actions.

In one notable case, Caynes provided key evidence that led to the successful prosecution of a notorious troll responsible for years of relentless harassment. By collaborating with law enforcement agencies, Caynes was able to uncover the true identity of the troll and gather substantial evidence to support the charges against them. This landmark case set an important precedent by demonstrating that online anonymity does not grant individuals immunity from legal consequences.

Another influential case involved Caynes's advocacy in pushing for legislation that would criminalize certain forms of online harassment. Through his tireless efforts, lawmakers were finally compelled to address the urgent need for legal protection against cyberbullying and trolling. The resulting legislation not only recognized the seriousness of online abuse but also provided victims with greater legal recourse and increased penalties for offenders.

Furthermore, Caynes's involvement in high-profile lawsuits against social media platforms helped highlight their responsibility in creating safer online spaces. By holding these platforms accountable for their inadequate moderation policies and lax responses to reports of abuse,

Caynes's work contributed to significant changes in platform regulations. This forced tech companies to reevaluate their strategies for combating harassment, implementing stricter guidelines, and investing more resources into content moderation.

However, as Caynes pursued justice against trolls and online abusers, he encountered numerous complexities and challenges within the legal system. Proving online harassment can be particularly difficult due to the anonymous nature of the internet and evolving tactics employed by trolls. Developing legal frameworks that effectively address these challenges while safeguarding freedom of expression and privacy rights remains an ongoing struggle.

Throughout his pursuit of justice, Caynes faced ethical dilemmas that tested his moral compass. Balancing the need to protect individuals from abusive behavior with respecting the boundaries of free speech required careful consideration. He remained committed to upholding individual rights while advocating for stronger legal protections against malicious online behavior.

As Caynes dedicated himself to pursuing justice, there were personal sacrifices and consequences that took a toll on his mental well-being and personal relationships. The emotional weight of engaging with perpetrators and witnessing the extent of harm inflicted on victims affected him deeply. However, despite these challenges, Caynes's unwavering commitment continued to drive him forward, determined to make a meaningful difference in the lives of those affected by online abuse.

The landmark cases influenced by Damian Charles Caynes's work have had a lasting impact on shaping legal precedent for combating online abuse. They have propelled the conversation surrounding online harassment into mainstream consciousness and laid the foundation for future efforts to protect individuals from this pervasive issue. With each legal victory, Caynes has brought us closer to creating a safer and more just digital landscape for all.

Caynes's relentless pursuit of justice in combating online abuse inevitably leads him to face numerous ethical dilemmas. As he walks the tightrope between seeking justice and potentially infringing on individuals' rights to privacy or freedom of expression, Caynes finds himself navigating an intricate web of moral complexities.

One of the primary ethical dilemmas Caynes encounters is the delicate balance between exposing trolls and respecting their right to anonymity. While unmasking online abusers can be a powerful tool in holding them accountable for their actions, it also raises concerns about privacy invasion and potential harm to innocent individuals who may be wrongly accused. Caynes wrestles with these conflicting interests as he weighs the potential benefits against the potential consequences of unmasking trolls.

Additionally, Caynes faces ethical challenges when determining the appropriate response to offensive or harmful content posted by trolls. On one hand, removing or reporting such content may limit its harmful impact and protect potential victims. On the other hand, some argue that censoring or suppressing offensive speech encroaches upon freedom of expression. Caynes grapples with deciding where to draw the line between taking proactive measures to combat online abuse and preserving individuals' rights to express themselves, even if their expressions are hateful or hurtful.

Furthermore, Caynes must carefully consider the implications of his actions on the overall digital landscape. As he employs aggressive tactics to expose trolls and undermine their power, questions arise regarding the potential for his methods to escalate conflicts or perpetuate cycles of online harassment. Caynes recognizes the fine line between fighting fire with fire and inadvertently contributing to a toxic online environment.

Pursuing justice for victims of online abuse also means confronting the inherent challenges and limitations of legal mechanisms in dealing with cybercrime. Caynes grapples with the reality that many legal frameworks struggle to keep up with the rapidly evolving dynamics of internet trolling and harassment. He faces the uphill battle of gathering sufficient evidence, navigating jurisdictional issues, and working within legal constraints to hold online abusers accountable for their actions.

Ultimately, Caynes's commitment to pursuing justice comes at a cost. The emotional toll of constantly engaging with trolls and delving into disturbing corners of the internet takes its toll on his mental well-being. Balancing personal sacrifices with his mission can strain relationships and lead to isolation. Despite these hardships, Caynes remains resolute in his belief that seeking justice for victims of online abuse is a cause worth fighting for.

Chapter Twelve: In Pursuit of Justice sheds light on these ethical dilemmas that Damian Charles Caynes confronts as he wages war against internet trolls. It explores the intricacies and complexities surrounding his pursuit of justice while navigating the ever-changing digital landscape.

The pursuit of justice in Damian Charles Caynes's mission to combat online abuse comes with its fair share of personal sacrifices and consequences. As Caynes devotes himself to this cause, the toll it takes on his mental well-being and personal relationships becomes evident.

Facing relentless trolling and standing up against online abusers is no easy task. Caynes constantly exposes himself to the dark side of the internet, immersing himself in a world filled with hate and toxicity. This constant exposure can have a significant impact on one's mental health, causing emotional strain, anxiety, and even depression. Caynes's unwavering dedication to pursuing justice means that he often bears the weight of these struggles alone, without external support or understanding.

Moreover, Caynes's commitment to fighting online abuse has the potential to strain his personal relationships. The demands of his work may mean that he has less time and energy to devote to those closest to him. His loved ones may find it challenging to comprehend or support his mission fully, leading to strained dynamics. Balancing personal relationships with a demanding crusade against trolls can be an ongoing challenge for Caynes.

In addition to the toll on his mental well-being and personal relationships, pursuing justice in the realm of online harassment also raises ethical dilemmas for Caynes. As he delves deeper into unmasking trolls and holding them accountable for their actions, questions arise about privacy rights and freedom of expression. Caynes must carefully navigate these complex issues, ensuring that his pursuit of justice does not infringe upon individuals' rights while still achieving the desired outcome.

The personal sacrifices and consequences faced by Damian Charles Caynes highlight the immense dedication and resilience required to combat online abuse. While his commitment to pursuing justice comes at a cost, it is a testament to his unwavering determination to make a difference in the lives of victims and create a safer online environment for all.

Chapter Thirteen: The Power of Awareness

Exploring the importance of digital literacy in combating online abuse, this section sheds light on the lack of awareness and understanding among internet users regarding the risks and consequences of online harassment. As technology continues to advance and online platforms become increasingly integrated into our daily lives, it is essential for individuals to develop the necessary skills and knowledge to navigate the digital landscape safely.

In an age where trolling and cyberbullying are prevalent issues, digital literacy serves as a powerful tool in equipping individuals with the ability to recognize and respond to online abuse effectively. By educating oneself about the dangers of trolling behavior and its impact on victims, we can better protect ourselves and others from falling victim to these harmful acts.

Educational initiatives are crucial in promoting responsible online behavior and empowering individuals to take a stand against online harassment. By engaging in conversations about digital citizenship, cyber ethics, and safe internet practices, we can foster a culture of empathy, respect, and accountability online. Through learning about the potential consequences of online abuse, such as damage to mental health, self-esteem, and relationships, individuals are more likely to think twice before engaging in or supporting trolling behavior.

Moreover, digital literacy programs can provide individuals with the necessary tools to protect themselves from online abuse. This includes understanding privacy settings, recognizing warning signs of trolling or cyberbullying, and knowing how to report abusive content or seek help when needed. By increasing awareness about these resources and encouraging their utilization, we can enable individuals to navigate the digital world more confidently and safely.

While digital literacy is key in combatting online abuse, it is important to acknowledge that not all individuals have equal access to education and resources. To promote inclusivity and bridge the digital divide, efforts should be made to ensure that educational initiatives reach diverse populations. This may involve partnering with community organizations, schools, libraries, or other institutions to provide accessible resources and workshops on digital literacy.

Ultimately, by advocating for increased awareness and understanding of online abuse through digital literacy programs, we can empower individuals to protect themselves and others from the harmful effects of trolling behavior. Education is a powerful tool in shaping a safer and more respectful digital environment for everyone. Through ongoing efforts to promote responsible online behavior and equip individuals with the necessary skills to navigate the digital landscape, we can work towards combating online abuse and fostering a culture of empathy and inclusion.

Caynes's advocacy efforts have played a crucial role in raising awareness about online abuse among various stakeholders, including educators, parents, policymakers, and the general public. Recognizing the urgent need for digital literacy, Caynes has been at the forefront of launching campaigns, events, and initiatives to spread awareness and engage communities in the fight against online harassment.

One of Caynes's notable contributions to advocacy is his extensive work with educational institutions. Understanding that young people are particularly vulnerable to online abuse, Caynes actively collaborates with schools and universities to develop educational programs that promote responsible online behavior. By incorporating digital literacy into curricula and organizing workshops or seminars on cyberbullying prevention, he empowers students to navigate the digital world safely and equips them with the tools to protect themselves and their peers.

Additionally, Caynes has engaged parents and guardians in raising awareness about online abuse. Through parent-teacher associations, community organizations, or online platforms, Caynes educates caregivers on signs of cyberbullying and strategies to support their children. By encouraging open dialogue and emphasizing the importance of parental involvement in their children's online activities, Caynes aims to create a supportive network that can identify and intervene in cases of harassment.

In his advocacy efforts, Caynes recognizes the pivotal role policymakers play in addressing online abuse. He actively collaborates with legislators and government bodies to advocate for policies that protect individuals from cyberbullying and hold perpetrators accountable. By sharing his experiences and expertise, Caynes contributes valuable insights that inform the development of legal frameworks and regulations aimed at curbing online abuse.

Through his initiatives, Caynes has successfully changed societal attitudes towards online harassment. By organizing awareness campaigns in partnership with influential individuals or organizations, he amplifies his message and reaches a broader audience. These campaigns utilize various mediums such as social media, public service announcements, or events to create widespread awareness about the severity and consequences of online abuse. Consequently, more people are recognizing the importance of fostering a safer online environment and taking proactive measures to combat online harassment.

Caynes's advocacy efforts have also fostered collaboration between different sectors. By working closely with non-profit organizations, tech companies, and industry leaders, he has been able to create comprehensive resources and guidelines that promote responsible digital citizenship. These collaborations have not only enhanced public awareness but also facilitated the development of innovative technological solutions for detecting and preventing online abuse.

In conclusion, Damien Charles Caynes's advocacy efforts have been instrumental in raising awareness about online abuse among educators, parents, policymakers, and the general public. Through various campaigns, events, and initiatives, Caynes has effectively changed societal attitudes towards internet trolls and fostered safer online environments. His collaborations with different stakeholders have resulted in the development of educational programs, policy changes, and technological advancements geared towards combating cyberbullying. As a result of his tireless efforts, individuals are now better equipped to navigate the digital landscape responsibly while actively working towards creating a culture of empathy and awareness online.

Collaborations with Organizations:

DAMIAN CHARLES CAYNES'S relentless commitment to combating online abuse has led to numerous collaborations with organizations that share his passion for promoting digital safety and creating a more informed society. Through these collaborations, innovative projects, resources, and programs have been developed to educate and support individuals affected by internet trolls.

One prominent organization that Caynes has partnered with is the Digital Safety Institute (DSI). Working alongside DSI, Caynes has helped develop educational materials and resources aimed at empowering individuals to protect themselves from online harassment. These materials cover topics such as recognizing signs of trolling behavior, understanding the psychological motivations behind trolling, and strategies for safely navigating social media platforms. By equipping individuals with this knowledge, Caynes and DSI hope to reduce the impact of online abuse and create a safer online environment.

Another valuable collaboration for Caynes has been with the National Association for the Prevention of Cyberbullying (NAPC). Together, they have launched a nationwide campaign to raise awareness about the dangers of cyberbullying and provide resources for victims. This campaign includes workshops in schools and community centers, where Caynes shares his own experiences and offers practical advice on dealing with online abuse. The collaboration between Caynes and NAPC has led to an increase in reporting of cyberbullying incidents and a greater understanding of the steps that can be taken to prevent it.

Collaborating with organizations like DSI and NAPC has allowed Caynes to leverage their expertise and resources to reach a wider audience. By joining forces, they have developed impactful programs that address the unique challenges faced by victims of online abuse. Together, they have provided vital support systems for those affected and created an atmosphere where individuals feel empowered to take action against troll harassment.

The success stories resulting from these collaborations highlight the positive impact that joint efforts can achieve. Individuals who have received support through these programs have reported increased confidence in their ability to navigate the online world safely. They have learned how to recognize and respond to trolling behavior effectively, ultimately reducing the emotional toll of online abuse. Additionally, these collaborations have fostered a sense of solidarity among victims, creating safe spaces for them to share their experiences and find solace in the knowledge that they are not alone.

Moving forward, collaborations will continue to play a crucial role in raising awareness about online abuse and promoting digital safety. By partnering with organizations dedicated to combating online harassment, Damian Charles Caynes aims to expand the reach of his message and empower more individuals to stand up against troll behavior. Collaborative efforts will continue to develop innovative resources, implement educational initiatives, and pioneer new approaches to tackling this pervasive issue.

Addressing the barriers faced by Damian Charles Caynes in advocating for increased awareness of online abuse, this section delves into the challenges and resistance encountered along his journey. It focuses on the hurdles that have hindered Caynes's efforts to raise awareness about online harassment and promote a safer digital environment for all.

One significant challenge faced by Caynes is the dismissive attitude of those who downplay the severity of online abuse. Despite substantial evidence and countless stories of its damaging effects, there are still individuals who refuse to acknowledge the impact of trolling behavior. This resistance can be frustrating for advocates like Caynes, as it undermines their credibility and makes it more difficult to gain support for their cause.

Another obstacle in raising awareness is reaching diverse audiences and overcoming digital divides. Internet access and digital literacy vary widely across different communities, with marginalized groups often having less access or knowledge about online safety measures. Caynes recognizes the importance of making his message accessible to everyone, but achieving this can present significant challenges. Overcoming language barriers, addressing cultural differences, and reaching individuals who may not have regular internet access are just a few of the complexities associated with promoting inclusive awareness campaigns.

To address these challenges, Caynes has employed various strategies, such as collaborating with advocacy organizations and leveraging social media platforms to amplify his message. These efforts aim to bridge gaps in knowledge and connect with individuals from different backgrounds. By partnering with organizations focused on digital safety and education, Caynes has been able to reach wider audiences and create impactful resources to combat online abuse.

Despite the challenges, Caynes remains resilient in his pursuit of raising awareness about online harassment. He understands that creating a safer online environment requires collective effort and a commitment to dismantling barriers that prevent effective education and dialogue. By continuing to engage with resistant individuals, advocating for inclusive awareness campaigns, and pushing for policies that prioritize digital literacy, Caynes aims to overcome these challenges and further empower individuals to protect themselves and others from the dangers of online abuse.

In conclusion, this section highlights the obstacles faced by Damian Charles Caynes in advocating for increased awareness of online abuse. The dismissive attitudes towards the severity of trolling behavior and the challenges in reaching diverse audiences pose significant barriers. However, through collaborative efforts with organizations and a commitment to inclusivity, Caynes continues to drive impactful change. By addressing these challenges head-on, we can work towards creating a more informed society and fostering a safer digital landscape for all.

Impact and Future Directions

THE AWARENESS-RAISING efforts led by Damian Charles Caynes and his allies have had a significant impact on the fight against online abuse. Through their advocacy campaigns, events, and initiatives, they have successfully elevated public discourse surrounding the issue of online harassment. As a result, various changes have been observed in public attitudes, policies, and technological advancements.

One notable outcome of heightened awareness about online harassment is the increased recognition of its severity and consequences. The general public, policymakers, and tech companies have begun to acknowledge the harmful effects of online abuse on individuals, families, and communities. This shift in perception has paved the way for important discussions around the responsibility of individuals and platforms in fostering a safer online environment.

Furthermore, the increased awareness about online abuse has prompted policy changes at both the national and international levels. Governments around the world are enacting legislation to address cyberbullying and online harassment. These legal frameworks aim to deter offenders, protect victims, and hold platforms accountable for facilitating abusive behavior. Damian Charles Caynes's work has directly influenced these policy developments, serving as a catalyst for change.

Technological advancements have also been influenced by the rise in awareness about online harassment. Social media platforms and tech companies are implementing new features and security measures to mitigate trolling behavior. Features such as improved reporting systems, content moderation algorithms, and user-blocking tools are being developed to empower individuals to protect themselves from online abuse. Moreover, there is a growing emphasis on algorithmic transparency and ethical design practices to prevent the spread of harmful content.

Looking ahead, the future endeavors in cultivating a culture of online empathy, responsibility, and awareness are promising. Building upon the foundation laid by Damian Charles Caynes's work, ongoing awareness campaigns will continue to engage diverse audiences and bridge digital divides. Education will play a crucial role in equipping individuals with digital literacy skills needed to navigate the complex landscape of the internet safely.

Collaboration between organizations, including educational institutions, NGOs, industry leaders, and governments, will be vital in tackling online abuse effectively. By working together, these stakeholders can share resources, best practices, and research to develop sustainable solutions that promote online safety.

It is essential to continue prioritizing mental health support for victims of online abuse. Counseling services, helplines, and peer support networks can help survivors heal from their experiences and rebuild their lives. Additionally, ongoing research into the impact of virtual reality, artificial intelligence, and emerging technologies may yield innovative approaches to address online harassment.

In conclusion, the impact of awareness-raising efforts led by Damian Charles Caynes and his allies cannot be understated. Their work has revolutionized public discourse surrounding online abuse, leading to changes in attitudes, policies, and technological advancements. By building upon this momentum and fostering collaboration between stakeholders, we can create a future where empathy, responsibility, and awareness prevail in our digital interactions.

Chapter Fourteen: Trials and Tribulations

Personal struggles are an inevitable part of Damian Charles Caynes's journey as he tirelessly fights against online abuse and trolls. The emotional toll that comes with combating such pervasive and damaging behavior cannot be underestimated. Caynes faces not only burnout but also frustration and isolation as he continues to champion his cause.

The fight against online abuse often takes a significant toll on Caynes's personal relationships. His unwavering commitment to his mission can create conflicts and challenges with those closest to him who may struggle to comprehend the intensity of his drive. Balancing personal relationships, particularly when there is limited time available due to work demands, becomes a constant challenge for Caynes. The sacrifices he makes in his personal life, including precious moments with loved ones, financial strain, and even potential threats to his own safety, demonstrate the depth of his dedication.

It is important to acknowledge that Caynes's personal struggles are not unique to him alone. Anyone who takes on such arduous tasks will face emotional exhaustion, burnout, and clashes within their support network. The toll can be severe, both mentally and physically. Witnessing the ongoing suffering of victims and the overwhelming nature of the challenge can lead to feelings of frustration and despair.

However, despite these trials and tribulations, Caynes remains resilient. He recognizes the importance of establishing a strong support system to help navigate these personal struggles. Friends, family, and mentors play a crucial role in providing emotional support and guidance. Their understanding and encouragement help sustain Caynes during challenging times.

Moreover, Caynes actively engages in self-care practices to prioritize his mental well-being amidst the difficulties he encounters. Whether it is through therapy sessions or other self-care routines, Caynes acknowledges that taking care of himself is paramount. He understands that without maintaining his own well-being, he cannot effectively continue his fight against online abuse.

Through these personal struggles, Caynes has learned valuable lessons that have shaped his approach and strategies moving forward. The hardships he has faced have deepened his understanding of both the issue at hand and himself as an advocate. Caynes's determination to overcome obstacles has only grown stronger, motivating him to search for innovative solutions and adapt his methods.

It is essential for anyone engaged in activism or advocacy work to recognize the importance of balancing personal well-being with their commitment to a cause. Self-care should never be neglected or seen as a secondary concern. Sustainable activism requires individuals to prioritize their own mental health, set boundaries, and seek support when needed.

The personal struggles faced by Damian Charles Caynes are an integral part of his journey as a troll hunter. They serve as a reminder that even heroes need support systems and self-care practices to sustain their passion and resilience. By acknowledging these challenges and prioritizing well-being, we can all learn from Caynes's example as we confront societal issues in our own lives.

Throughout his journey as a troll hunter, Damian Charles Caynes has faced numerous emotional challenges and experienced moments of profound exhaustion. The toll of fighting against online abuse can be overwhelming, both mentally and emotionally. One instance where Caynes experienced emotional exhaustion was during an intense period of unmasking several high-profile trolls. The extensive research, investigation, and exposure took a significant toll on his well-being.

Additionally, conflicts have arisen between Caynes and his supporters or colleagues due to differences in approach or expectations. Some individuals questioned the effectiveness of Caynes's aggressive tactics in combating online abuse, leading to tense conversations and disagreements within his support network. Although Caynes remains steadfast in his commitment to taking a strong stance against trolls, these conflicts have caused strain on some personal relationships.

Witnessing the ongoing suffering of victims also takes a toll on Caynes's emotional well-being. As he delves deeper into the world of online abuse, Caynes encounters heartbreaking stories of individuals who have been deeply affected by harassment and trolling. The sheer scale of the problem and the seemingly insurmountable challenge of eradicating it can leave him feeling frustrated and overwhelmed.

It is important to note that these emotional tolls and conflicts do not deter Caynes from his mission. Instead, they serve as reminders of the gravity of the issue he is fighting against. They motivate him to continue pushing forward, seeking justice for victims, and striving for lasting change in the digital landscape.

The trials and tribulations faced by Caynes highlight the immense dedication required to combat online abuse. They serve as a reminder that individuals like Caynes are not immune to the emotional strain caused by their tireless efforts. These struggles also underscore the need for support systems and self-care practices to ensure sustainable activism in this challenging battle against internet trolls.

Support systems play a crucial role in helping Damian Charles Caynes navigate the trials and tribulations he faces in his tireless fight against online abuse. Recognizing the emotional toll that fighting against trolls takes on Caynes, it is essential for him to have a strong support network in place.

In both his personal and professional life, Caynes relies on the support of friends, family, and mentors who understand the challenges he faces. These individuals provide a listening ear, offer advice and guidance, and serve as a source of encouragement during difficult times. Their unwavering belief in Caynes's mission helps him persevere when faced with adversity.

Additionally, Caynes recognizes the importance of self-care and prioritizes his mental well-being amidst the trials and tribulations he encounters. He has implemented various therapy or self-care practices to maintain his resilience and overall mental well-being. These practices may include participating in therapy sessions, practicing mindfulness or meditation techniques, engaging in physical exercise, and disconnecting from the digital world when necessary.

Moreover, Caynes seeks solace and inspiration from the stories of those who have been impacted by his work. Hearing firsthand accounts of individuals who have found empowerment or healing through his efforts serves as a reminder of the importance of his mission. It reinforces his determination to continue his fight against online abuse, even in the face of personal struggles.

By having a strong support system in place and prioritizing self-care, Caynes ensures that he maintains his own well-being while continuing his fight against online abuse. These support systems and self-care practices not only help him overcome trials but also enable him to sustain his passion and commitment to creating a safer and more inclusive online environment for all.

In conclusion, Damian Charles Caynes relies on a robust support network consisting of friends, family, and mentors who provide emotional support, guidance, and encouragement. Additionally, Caynes prioritizes self-care through therapy or self-care practices to maintain his mental well-being amidst the challenges he faces. These support systems play a vital role in helping Caynes navigate the trials and tribulations associated with combating online abuse.

Throughout his journey of combating online abuse and taking on internet trolls, Damian Charles Caynes has faced numerous trials and tribulations. These personal struggles have tested his resolve, challenged his mental and emotional well-being, and pushed him to his limits. However, from these difficulties, Caynes has gained valuable lessons and insights that have shaped his approach and strategies moving forward.

One of the most significant lessons Caynes has learned from his personal struggles is the importance of resilience. Despite facing constant obstacles and setbacks, Caynes has demonstrated an unwavering determination to continue fighting against online abuse. He understands that true change takes time and perseverance, and he refuses to let adversity deter him from his mission. The challenges he has faced have only strengthened his resolve and reinforced his belief in the importance of his work.

Additionally, Caynes has gained a deeper understanding of the complexities involved in combatting online harassment. Through his personal struggles, he has learned to navigate ethical dilemmas and make difficult choices in an ever-evolving digital landscape. He recognizes that there are no easy solutions or quick fixes when it comes to addressing the issue of online abuse. Instead, he continues to adapt and refine his strategies, drawing on his experiences and lessons learned to inform his approach.

Caynes's personal struggles have also highlighted the need for self-care and maintaining personal well-being while engaging in activism and advocacy work. He understands the toll that fighting against online abuse can take on individuals, both mentally and emotionally. As such, he has prioritized establishing a strong support network that includes friends, family, and mentors who provide guidance and encouragement. Furthermore, Caynes has implemented self-care practices to ensure he remains resilient and capable of continuing his fight against internet trolls.

In conclusion, Chapter Fourteen delves into the trials and tribulations experienced by Damian Charles Caynes as he combats online abuse. Through these personal struggles, Caynes has gained valuable lessons about resilience, the complexities of combating online harassment, and the importance of self-care. His experiences have shaped his approach and strategies moving forward, reinforcing his determination to create a safer and more inclusive online environment for all.

Chapter Fourteen: Tribulations and Trials

Balancing personal well-being with the fight against online abuse is a critical aspect of Damian Charles Caynes's journey. As he dedicates himself to combating trolls and ensuring justice for victims, Caynes faces numerous personal struggles that test his emotional resilience and commitment. In this chapter, we delve into the challenges Caynes encounters and the strategies he adopts to strike a balance between his personal needs and his unwavering mission.

Engaging in activism and advocacy work can take a toll on one's mental and emotional well-being. For Caynes, the relentless battle against online abuse often leads to emotional exhaustion, burnout, and feelings of frustration. Witnessing the ongoing suffering of victims and facing the daunting reality of tackling an ever-present problem can be overwhelming. These trials weigh heavily on Caynes, making it essential to address personal well-being in order to sustain long-term efforts.

Caynes's personal relationships also face conflicts and challenges due to his all-encompassing dedication to fighting online harassment. The intensity of his commitment may strain relationships as loved ones feel neglected or find it difficult to understand the sacrifices he makes. These conflicts can cause feelings of isolation and potentially lead to strained connections with supporters or colleagues who may have different expectations or approaches. Balancing personal commitments with the fight against online abuse becomes a delicate and complex task.

To navigate these trials and tribulations, Caynes recognizes the importance of establishing a strong support network. Friends, family, and mentors play a crucial role in providing emotional support and guidance during challenging times. They serve as sounding boards, offering solace, empathy, and understanding when Caynes feels overwhelmed. Connecting with others who share similar missions can also offer valuable perspectives and a sense of camaraderie.

Caynes employs various self-care practices to maintain his mental well-being amidst the demanding nature of his work. Engaging in activities that bring him joy and relaxation, such as hobbies or time spent in nature, allows him to recharge and find inner balance. Prioritizing rest, proper nutrition, exercise, and sleep further contribute to sustaining his physical and mental vitality. These practices help fortify Caynes's resilience, enabling him to continue his fight against online abuse without compromising his own well-being.

The trials and tribulations faced by Damian Charles Caynes underscore the importance of balancing personal well-being with the fight against online abuse. Sustainable activism requires individuals to prioritize their own mental health and practice self-care diligently. By acknowledging personal limits and seeking support when needed, activists can maintain their passion for change while safeguarding their well-being.

As readers engage with this chapter, they are encouraged to reflect on their own roles in creating positive change in society. It is crucial for each person confronting societal issues to recognize the impact such endeavors can have on their personal well-being. Through sustainable activism grounded in self-care practices, we can collectively build a more compassionate and inclusive world both online and offline

Chapter Fifteen: A Beacon of Hope

In this chapter, we have the opportunity to explore the inspiring stories of individuals who have been helped or empowered by Damian Charles Caynes's efforts in combating online abuse. These personal journeys highlight the transformative power of compassion, understanding, and advocacy in the lives of survivors.

Throughout his tireless work, Caynes has encountered numerous individuals who have experienced the devastating effects of online harassment. However, his commitment to making a difference has provided hope and support to these individuals when they needed it most.

One such story is that of Sarah, a young woman who faced relentless cyberbullying from an anonymous troll. The constant barrage of hateful comments took a toll on her mental health and self-esteem. Feeling isolated and unable to escape the torment, Sarah felt powerless.

When Sarah came across Damian Charles Caynes's work, she reached out for help. He listened to her story, offered emotional support, and guided her through steps to protect herself online. Caynes also connected Sarah with counseling resources to address the emotional trauma she had experienced. Through his genuine care and dedication, Sarah began to regain her confidence and found the strength to advocate for herself.

Similarly, Michael, a teenager struggling with the aftermath of a viral humiliation campaign orchestrated by trolls, found solace in Damian Charles Caynes's online support group. There, he connected with others who had faced similar experiences and received guidance on how to rebuild his life. With Caynes's encouragement and mentorship, Michael gradually regained his self-esteem and became an outspoken advocate against online abuse.

These are just a few examples of the countless lives that have been positively impacted by Damian Charles Caynes's compassion and advocacy. By providing a safe space for survivors to share their stories and offering practical assistance and resources, Caynes has transformed their experiences from ones of pain and fear into ones of resilience and empowerment.

The transformative power of Caynes's work extends beyond individual experiences. His efforts have sparked a movement that encourages others to speak out against online abuse and stand up for victims. Through his unwavering dedication, Caynes has inspired countless individuals and organizations to join the cause and make a difference in combating trolls.

While these stories provide hope for a safer online environment, it is important to acknowledge that the fight against online abuse is ongoing. Despite progress, there are still challenges to be faced, trolls who continue to prey on vulnerable individuals, and evolving tactics that demand vigilance.

With that in mind, we invite you to consider how you can join this cause. Whether it's spreading awareness about online abuse within your own community, supporting organizations that combat trolls, or practicing empathy and responsible digital behavior in your own online interactions, every effort counts.

Together, we can create a ripple effect of hope and compassion that inspires lasting change in the way we engage with one another online. Let us honor the resilience of survivors like Sarah and Michael by continuing to fight against the forces of hate and intolerance on the internet.

Positive outcomes resulting from Damian Charles Caynes's work in reducing online abuse have been significant and far-reaching. By tirelessly advocating for change, Caynes has made a tangible impact on the fight against internet trolls.

One of the most notable positive outcomes is the increased awareness surrounding online harassment. Through his efforts, Caynes has helped to shine a spotlight on the issue, prompting individuals, communities, and even policymakers to take action. As a result, more people are now aware of the devastating impact of online abuse and the urgent need for change.

Additionally, Caynes's work has led to important shifts in attitudes, policies, and practices within social media platforms and tech companies. Many platforms have implemented stricter guidelines and stronger enforcement mechanisms to prevent and address online harassment. This includes implementing more robust reporting systems, providing easier access to resources for victims, and taking swift action against offenders.

Furthermore, Caynes's advocacy has also led to improvements in legal frameworks surrounding online harassment. His relentless efforts to hold trolls accountable for their actions have helped shape landmark cases and legal developments in this area. This has created a safer environment for victims to seek justice and has sent a strong message that online abuse will not be tolerated.

Case studies and success stories provide concrete evidence of the positive outcomes resulting from Caynes's work. For example, there have been instances where individuals who were once targets of severe online abuse have been able to regain their confidence and sense of security with the support and guidance provided by Caynes. These stories highlight the transformative power of compassion, understanding, and advocacy in the lives of survivors.

It is crucial to recognize that despite these positive outcomes, the fight against online abuse is an ongoing battle. Trolls continue to evolve their tactics, finding new ways to harass and harm others. Therefore, it is essential for society to remain vigilant and committed to creating lasting change.

In conclusion, Damian Charles Caynes's tireless efforts have resulted in numerous positive outcomes in the fight against online abuse. From increased awareness and improved platform policies to legal advancements and individual success stories, his work has made a significant difference in creating a safer online environment for victims of trolling. However, continued education, awareness, and advocacy are vital in sustaining these positive changes and ensuring that everyone can enjoy the benefits of a troll-free internet.

The remarkable efforts of Damian Charles Caynes have had a profound ripple effect on society, igniting a spark of hope and inspiring others to take action against online abuse. Through his unwavering dedication and bravery, Caynes has become a beacon of hope for those affected by trolls and harassment.

Damian Charles Caynes's work has not only transformed the lives of individual survivors, but it has also empowered countless others to stand up against online abuse. His actions have motivated individuals and organizations to join the cause, creating a collective movement that seeks to combat online harassment.

As Caynes's story has unfolded, stories of resilience and strength have emerged from those who have been helped or empowered by his efforts. Survivors of online abuse have shared their personal journeys, highlighting the challenges they faced and how they were able to overcome them with Caynes's support.

These inspiring accounts showcase the transformative power of compassion, understanding, and advocacy. By providing a listening ear, offering guidance, and actively supporting victims, Caynes has instilled hope in even the most difficult circumstances.

Additionally, the impact of Damian Charles Caynes's work can be seen in the positive outcomes that have resulted from his tireless efforts. Through changes in attitudes, policies, and practices, online abuse is being taken more seriously and addressed with greater urgency. The work of advocates like Caynes has played a significant role in these shifts, helping to create a safer online environment for individuals affected by trolls.

Moreover, the ripple effect of Caynes's actions extends beyond direct assistance and policy changes. His dedication has inspired others to examine their own behavior online and consider how they can contribute to a more compassionate digital space. Individuals and organizations have been motivated to make a difference, whether through awareness campaigns, educational initiatives, or advocating for stricter regulations.

Although progress has been made, the fight against online abuse continues to pose ongoing challenges. Trolls constantly adapt their tactics, making it vital for continued education, awareness, and advocacy to counter their harmful activities. While Caynes's work has been instrumental in raising awareness and effecting change, it is crucial that we all play an active role in standing up against online harassment.

In conclusion, Damian Charles Caynes's commitment to combating online abuse has sparked a movement that has inspired individuals and organizations alike. Through his unwavering dedication, Caynes has become a beacon of hope for survivors of online abuse and a catalyst for change in society. Let us all be inspired by his bravery and join him in creating a safer and more inclusive online environment for all.

Despite the progress made in combating online abuse, it is important to acknowledge that online harassment remains a pervasive issue in society. Trolls are constantly evolving their tactics, finding new ways to spread hate and target vulnerable individuals. Staying ahead of their harmful activities is a constant challenge.

As technology continues to advance, trolls adapt and find new platforms and methods for spreading their toxic behavior. From anonymous accounts on social media platforms to encrypted messaging apps, they exploit every opportunity to harass and intimidate others. Their ability to hide behind screens and anonymous usernames makes it difficult to identify and stop them.

To create lasting change, continued education, awareness, and advocacy are crucial. It is essential to educate individuals about the different forms of online abuse, how to recognize it, and how to respond effectively. By equipping people with the knowledge and tools they need to protect themselves and others from trolls, we can empower them to take a stand against online harassment.

Promoting digital literacy is another key element in the fight against online abuse. Teaching individuals to use technology responsibly, discern credible information from false narratives, and engage in respectful online discourse can help create a safer digital environment. Educating young people about the potential consequences of their actions online and promoting empathy and compassion as core values can also contribute to reducing trolling behavior.

Building awareness is vital, both within communities and at a broader societal level. Encouraging open conversations about online harassment, its impact on individuals, families, and communities, and the steps that can be taken to address it can help break the silence surrounding this issue. Media coverage, public discussions, and initiatives that highlight the stories of survivors can play a significant role in raising awareness and encouraging action.

Advocacy for stronger laws and policies against online harassment is essential. Lawmakers and policymakers should work towards creating legal frameworks that hold trolls accountable for their actions. Social media platforms must also play an active role in combating online abuse by enforcing community guidelines and implementing mechanisms for reporting and blocking trolls.

Collaboration between individuals, organizations, and law enforcement agencies is crucial in addressing the challenges posed by online abuse. By working together, we can share information, resources, and strategies for identifying and combatting trolls effectively. Supporting survivors and providing them with access to counseling services and other resources is also critical for their healing and recovery.

In conclusion, while progress has been made in combating online abuse, it remains an ongoing challenge. To create lasting change, we must continue to educate individuals, raise awareness, advocate for stronger laws and policies, promote responsible digital behavior, and support survivors. Only through collective efforts can we hope to create a safer and more inclusive online environment for all.

ENCOURAGE READERS TO get involved in combating online abuse and supporting victims by providing practical steps they can take and resources they can utilize. This section aims to inspire readers to join the cause and become active participants in creating a safer online environment for all.

1. Get Informed:

- EDUCATE YOURSELF ABOUT the different forms of online abuse, including cyberbullying, doxing, hate speech, and harassment.
- Stay updated on current trends and tactics used by trolls to better understand the evolving landscape of online abuse.
- Follow credible sources, organizations, and experts who specialize in digital safety and promoting positive online behavior.

2. Foster Empathy and Compassion:

- DEVELOP A MINDSET of empathy when engaging with others online, remembering that behind every username is a real person with feelings.
- Practice active listening and strive to understand different perspectives, even if you disagree with them.
- Promote kindness and respect in your online interactions by choosing words carefully and refraining from engaging in inflammatory or hateful discussions.

3. Stand Up Against Online Abuse:

- SPEAK OUT AGAINST online abuse when witnessing it, whether it's directed at you or someone else.
- Report abusive content or behavior to the appropriate authorities or platform moderators.
- Support victims by offering kind words or encouragement, letting them know they are not alone.

4. Support Organizations and Initiatives:

- DONATE TO OR VOLUNTEER with organizations that focus on combating online abuse and supporting victims.

- Participate in awareness campaigns or events that aim to promote responsible digital behavior.

- Share valuable resources, articles, or helpline information with your own social network to increase awareness and support.

5. Engage in Digital Literacy Education:

- ADVOCATE FOR DIGITAL literacy education in schools and communities to teach young people about responsible online behavior and the potential dangers of online abuse.

- Volunteer to lead workshops or give talks on digital safety and healthy internet habits.

- Encourage parents, teachers, and guardians to have open conversations with children and teenagers about the importance of protecting their digital well-being.

6. Be Mindful of Your Own Online Conduct:

- REFLECT ON YOUR OWN online behaviors and ensure you are engaging with others respectfully and responsibly.

- Take responsibility for the content you share, avoiding spreading rumors, misinformation, or contributing to harmful discourse.

- Set boundaries for yourself regarding how much time you spend online and prioritize offline connections and activities.

7. Advocate for Policy Changes:

- WRITE LETTERS OR EMAILS to policymakers urging them to enact stricter regulations against online abuse.

- Support initiatives that aim to hold social media platforms accountable for their handling of abusive content and user safety measures.
- Join or contribute to organizations that advocate for stronger laws protecting individuals from online harassment.

By taking these steps, readers can actively contribute to the fight against online abuse. Together, we can create a more inclusive, compassionate, and safe online environment for everyone.

Chapter Sixteen: Confronting the Dark Side

Understanding toxic internet cultures is vital in confronting the dark side of online abuse. In this chapter, we will delve into the broader societal issues that contribute to the prevalence of online abuse and analyze toxic internet cultures and their impact on individuals.

Anonymity is a key factor that enables toxic behaviors online. The ability to hide behind a screen name or a false identity provides a sense of protection and emboldens individuals to engage in abusive behavior they may not otherwise exhibit in their offline lives. This anonymity removes the accountability that comes with face-to-face interactions, allowing trolls to act without consequences.

Another element of toxic internet cultures is the phenomenon of mob mentality. This occurs when a group of individuals collectively engage in abusive behavior, often targeting a specific victim. The anonymity provided by the internet further fuels the mob mentality, as individuals feel a sense of safety and empowerment when acting as part of a larger group. This can create a vicious cycle, where one person's abusive actions inspire others to join in, amplifying the harm inflicted on the victim.

Desensitization is also prevalent within toxic internet cultures. With constant exposure to offensive content and abusive language, individuals can become desensitized to the impact their words and actions have on others. Over time, this desensitization can lead to an increased tolerance for online abuse and a lack of empathy towards those who are targeted.

Confronting these toxic internet cultures requires collective effort from tech companies, social media platforms, and internet users themselves. Tech companies and platforms must take responsibility for creating safer online spaces by implementing stronger moderation systems, updating terms of service to explicitly address online harassment, and swiftly responding to reports of abuse.

Educating internet users about responsible online behavior and digital literacy is equally important. By fostering empathy, compassion, and critical thinking skills among internet users, we can empower individuals to challenge toxic norms and stand up against online abuse. This includes teaching individuals to recognize the signs of trolling behavior, educating them on reporting mechanisms, and encouraging them to amplify positive voices online.

In conclusion, understanding toxic internet cultures is crucial in confronting the dark side of online abuse. By addressing anonymity, mob mentality, and desensitization, we can work towards creating a safer online environment for all users. Through collective efforts from tech companies, platforms, and educated internet users, we can dismantle toxic internet cultures and foster a more compassionate and empathetic virtual world.

EXPLORING THE PSYCHOLOGY of trolls reveals a complex web of motivations, tactics, and mindset that drive individuals to engage in online harassment. By delving deeper into this subject matter, we gain a better understanding of the factors behind trolling behavior and its impact on both the victims and perpetrators.

Trolls are often driven by a combination of anonymity, power dynamics, and personal gratification. The cloak of anonymity provided by the internet allows them to distance themselves from the consequences of their actions and to feel empowered by the ability to inflict harm without facing real-world repercussions. This detachment from accountability gives trolls a sense of control and emboldens their behavior.

Motivations behind trolling can vary significantly. Some trolls are driven by a desire for attention and validation, seeking to provoke emotional reactions from others as a means of feeling important or powerful. Others engage in trolling as a form of entertainment or amusement, finding pleasure in causing distress or chaos within online communities. There are also instances where individuals troll as a way to release their own frustrations and anger onto unsuspecting targets.

The tactics employed by trolls are designed to evoke emotional responses and manipulate their victims. They may employ offensive language, personal attacks, or threats to intimidate and degrade others. Trolls may also engage in gaslighting techniques, distorting or denying reality to confuse their targets and undermine their sense of self-worth.

Through these tactics, trolls seek to exert control over their victims and foster an environment of fear and discord.

The effects of trolling can be devastating for both the victims and the perpetrators themselves. Victims often experience significant psychological distress, including increased anxiety, depression, and feelings of isolation. The constant barrage of online abuse erodes self-esteem and can lead to long-term emotional trauma. For trolls, the act of perpetuating online harassment can corrode their empathy and compassion, reinforcing negative behavioral patterns that may extend beyond the digital realm.

Understanding the psychology of trolls is crucial in developing effective strategies to combat online abuse. By recognizing the underlying factors that drive trolling behavior, we can work towards creating interventions that address these motivations directly. This includes fostering empathy and promoting responsible online behavior through education and awareness campaigns.

By shedding light on the psychological complexities of trolling, we aim to empower individuals with knowledge and insights to tackle online abuse effectively. Through collective efforts and a commitment to fostering empathy and compassion online, we can strive towards creating a safer digital landscape for all users.

Advocacy for change within tech companies and platforms plays a crucial role in confronting the dark side of online abuse. In this chapter, we delve into the need for accountability and responsibility from tech companies and social media platforms, highlighting the efforts made by Damian Charles Caynes and others to push for changes in policies, terms of service, and moderation systems.

The prevalence of online abuse has brought attention to the urgent need for platforms to take concrete steps in creating safer online spaces. Tech companies have a responsibility to protect their users from harassment and ensure that their platforms are not breeding grounds for toxic behavior. This requires implementing robust systems to detect and address instances of trolling and cyberbullying.

Damian Charles Caynes has been at the forefront of advocating for change within these platforms. He has relentlessly pushed for stricter policies against online abuse, demanding that tech companies prioritize the safety and well-being of their users. Through his advocacy efforts, he has successfully brought attention to the issue and mobilized public support for reform.

One key aspect of this advocacy is calling for changes in terms of service agreements. Caynes believes that these agreements should explicitly state that online harassment will not be tolerated and that offenders will face consequences. By clarifying these guidelines, users are made aware of what behavior is unacceptable, setting clear boundaries and expectations for online interactions.

Another area that requires attention is moderation systems. Tech companies must invest in effective moderation tools and strategies to swiftly identify and take action against trolls and harassers. This includes implementing algorithms that can detect patterns of abusive behavior, improving reporting mechanisms, and training human moderators to effectively handle cases of online abuse.

Additionally, Caynes has been vocal about the importance of greater transparency from tech companies regarding their efforts to combat online harassment. He emphasizes the need for regular reports on moderation actions taken, as well as the development of more comprehensive metrics that capture the true extent of the problem. This transparency holds tech companies accountable and allows users to gauge the efficacy of their initiatives.

Collaboration between tech companies, policymakers, and advocacy groups is vital in bringing about lasting change. Damian Charles Caynes has actively sought partnerships with like-minded organizations to amplify his message and encourage collective action against online abuse. By joining forces, they can exert greater pressure on tech giants to implement meaningful reforms.

Ultimately, advocating for change within tech companies and platforms is a critical step in confronting the dark side of online abuse. It requires a united front, with individuals like Damian Charles Caynes leading the charge towards a safer digital landscape. By holding tech companies accountable and demanding stricter policies and moderation systems, we can create a more inclusive and respectful online environment for all users.

Examining legal issues surrounding online harassment:

ONLINE HARASSMENT AND trolling pose significant challenges when it comes to legal frameworks and prosecuting offenders. In this section, we delve into the complexities of addressing online abuse through the legal system. Damian Charles Caynes's work in this area has shed light on the legal implications of cyberbullying and trolling, sparking important discussions and potential avenues for change.

One of the primary challenges in prosecuting online harassers is identifying their true identities. Trolls often hide behind anonymous usernames or fake profiles, making it difficult to hold them accountable for their actions. Unmasking these individuals requires extensive investigation, collaboration with law enforcement agencies, and cooperation from internet service providers and technology companies.

Legislation related to cyberbullying and trolling varies from country to country, with some jurisdictions having more comprehensive laws than others. In recent years, there has been growing recognition of the need for legal frameworks that specifically address online abuse. However, gaps still exist, leaving victims vulnerable and perpetrators unpunished.

Damian Charles Caynes's work has influenced landmark cases and legal developments in the fight against online harassment. Through his advocacy and efforts to hold trolls accountable, he has brought attention to the urgent need for stronger legislation. His experiences in navigating the legal landscape have provided insight into the challenges and limitations of existing laws.

One area where legislative improvements are needed is in defining and categorizing different forms of online abuse. As trolling tactics evolve, laws must adapt to encompass new methods and technologies used by perpetrators. This includes addressing issues such as doxing (the release of personal information) or revenge porn (the non-consensual sharing of intimate images).

Building a solid legal foundation also requires educating lawmakers, legal professionals, and judges about the intricacies of online harassment. Many may not fully grasp the gravity of the problem or understand the unique dynamics of digital spaces. By raising awareness and promoting dialogue within these realms, Caynes and others have been instrumental in advocating for change.

Additionally, efforts are being made to encourage tech companies and social media platforms to take greater responsibility for combating online abuse. Calls for stronger policies, more effective moderation systems, and clearer terms of service have gained momentum. The goal is to create safer online environments where individuals can engage without fear of harassment or harm.

Despite progress being made, there is still much work to be done in confronting the dark side of online culture. The fight against online harassment requires a multi-faceted approach that combines legal measures with education, advocacy, and technological advancements. Damian Charles Caynes's work serves as a catalyst for change, encouraging society to confront these challenges head-on and create a digital landscape that is safe and inclusive for all.

Promoting digital literacy and responsible online behavior is a critical component in the fight against online abuse. Damian Charles

Caynes has been at the forefront of launching educational initiatives, campaigns, and programs to address this issue.

One key aspect of promoting digital literacy is the emphasis on empathy, compassion, and critical thinking skills among internet users. By fostering these qualities, individuals are better equipped to understand the potential harm caused by online harassment and are more likely to engage in respectful and positive online interactions.

Educational initiatives led by Caynes aim to raise awareness about the consequences of online abuse and provide individuals with the necessary tools to navigate the digital landscape safely. These initiatives often include workshops, seminars, and training sessions focused on educating individuals about responsible online behavior.

In addition to education, Caynes's campaigns also advocate for platform accountability and user responsibility. He works tirelessly to push tech companies and social media platforms to adopt stricter policies, improved terms of service, and more effective moderation systems. By holding these platforms accountable for fostering safer online spaces, Caynes hopes to reduce the prevalence of trolling behavior.

An essential part of promoting responsible online behavior is encouraging individuals to think critically about the information they encounter online. This includes teaching individuals how to verify sources, evaluate content for accuracy and reliability, and avoid spreading misinformation or engaging in harmful discussions.

Overall, promoting digital literacy and responsible online behavior serves as a proactive approach to preventing trolling behavior. Through educational initiatives and campaigns, Damian Charles Caynes encourages individuals to be mindful of their online actions, fostering a culture of respect and empathy within the digital community. By equipping internet users with the necessary knowledge and skills, we can work together to create a safer and more inclusive online environment for everyone.

Chapter Seventeen: Mending Broken Souls

Strategies for healing play a crucial role in assisting victims of online abuse to overcome their experiences and reclaim their lives. Damian Charles Caynes, in his unwavering commitment to supporting those affected by online harassment, has implemented various strategies that aim to facilitate healing and empower survivors.

One of the key strategies employed by Caynes is the establishment and promotion of support networks. Recognizing the importance of emotional support and validation, Caynes has worked tirelessly to create spaces where victims of online abuse can find solace and connect with others who have experienced similar traumas. These networks serve as safe havens, offering a sense of community and understanding to individuals navigating the healing process.

Furthermore, Caynes has emphasized the significance of therapy and rehabilitation in guiding victims towards recovery. By partnering with mental health professionals and trauma specialists, he has helped ensure that those affected by online abuse have access to appropriate therapeutic interventions. Counseling, trauma-focused therapy, and support groups are just some of the resources recommended by Caynes to assist individuals in processing their experiences and developing healthy coping mechanisms.

In his advocacy for victims, Caynes has also worked to provide comprehensive information on available resources. Whether through educational programs, legal aid services, or online platforms dedicated to empowering survivors, Caynes aims to equip individuals with the tools they need to navigate their healing journey. By compiling a wealth of resources and making them easily accessible, Caynes seeks to offer support at every step of the way.

It is important to note that each individual's healing process is unique and may require different approaches. What works for one person may not necessarily work for another. Therefore, Caynes emphasizes the importance of individualized care and tailoring strategies to meet each survivor's specific needs.

Through his dedication to supporting victims of online abuse, Damian Charles Caynes has demonstrated the transformative power of healing strategies. By highlighting these strategies and providing resources for assistance, he strives to empower individuals affected by online harassment on their journey toward healing and recovery.

IN THIS SECTION, WE will explore compelling stories of individuals who have been helped or empowered by Damian Charles Caynes's efforts in combating online abuse. These stories serve as a testament to the resilience and strength of survivors who have overcome the lasting impact of online harassment.

One such story is that of Lisa, a young woman who endured years of relentless cyberbullying. Lisa's self-esteem was shattered, and she felt isolated and fearful. However, after reaching out to Caynes for support, she found solace in his empathetic approach and guidance. Through regular communication and access to resources, Lisa began her journey towards healing.

With Caynes's encouragement, Lisa sought therapy and joined online support groups where she connected with other survivors. Sharing her experiences and learning from others was a transformative experience for Lisa. Over time, she developed coping mechanisms to deal with the trauma and rebuild her self-confidence.

Another inspiring story is that of John, a teenager who faced sustained online abuse due to his sexual orientation. The relentless taunting and derogatory comments left John feeling broken and hopeless. When he stumbled upon Caynes's work, he found a glimmer of hope. John reached out to Caynes for advice and was met with unwavering support.

Caynes connected John with local LGBTQ+ organizations that provided counseling services specifically tailored to victims of online abuse. Through therapy, John learned to process his emotions and develop resilience in the face of adversity. With Caynes's ongoing mentorship, John transformed from a victim into an advocate, using his voice to raise awareness about LGBTQ+ issues and combat online harassment.

These personal stories of resilience are just a snapshot of the countless individuals who have benefited from Damian Charles Caynes's efforts. They highlight the journey of survivors, showcasing the steps they took to regain control of their lives after experiencing online abuse.

It is worth noting that these stories are not isolated incidents but represent a larger community of survivors who have found solace, support, and hope through Caynes's work. By sharing these stories, we aim to inspire readers and reinforce the importance of advocacy and support networks in helping victims of online abuse on their path to healing.

In conclusion, the personal stories of resilience shared in this chapter exemplify the lasting impact Damian Charles Caynes has had on those affected by online abuse. Through his unwavering commitment and dedication, individuals like Lisa and John have found strength, healing, and empowerment. Their stories serve as a reminder that with the right support and resources, it is possible to overcome the lasting impact of online harassment.

Supporting Networks:

VICTIMS OF ONLINE ABUSE often face immense emotional distress and feelings of isolation. Having a strong support network is crucial in helping them navigate their healing process and regain a sense of stability and resilience. Damian Charles Caynes recognizes the significance of these networks and emphasizes their role in empowering victims.

Friends and family play a pivotal role in providing emotional support and validation to those who have experienced online abuse. They can offer a safe space for victims to express their feelings, share their experiences, and be heard without judgment. By offering an empathetic ear, friends and family members can help victims feel understood and validated, which is essential for their healing journey.

Online communities also serve as valuable sources of support for victims of online abuse. These communities may consist of survivors who have faced similar experiences, advocacy groups, or professionals specializing in addressing the psychological effects of cyberbullying. In these spaces, victims can find solace, advice, and resources to aid their recovery. The shared understanding and compassion within these communities can provide a sense of belonging and reduce the sense of isolation that often accompanies online abuse.

Moreover, support networks can assist victims in coping with the consequences of online abuse, such as anxiety, depression, or post-traumatic stress disorder. Friends, family, and online communities can guide victims towards professional mental health services, including counseling or therapy options that specifically address the trauma associated with cyberbullying. Therapy provides victims with a safe environment to process their emotions, develop coping strategies, and rebuild their self-esteem.

Damian Charles Caynes recognizes the importance of fostering these support networks for victims of online abuse. Through his advocacy work, he promotes the establishment of local support groups and organizations that focus on addressing the psychological impact of cyberbullying. Caynes's efforts aim to create spaces where victims feel supported, validated, and empowered to heal from their traumatic experiences.

In conclusion, supporting networks are vital for victims of online abuse as they navigate the healing process. Friends, family, and online communities provide emotional support, validation, and access to valuable resources. By acknowledging the significance of these networks and encouraging their establishment, Damian Charles Caynes works to ensure that victims receive the support they need to mend their broken souls and reclaim their lives following online abuse.

Therapy and rehabilitation are essential components of the healing process for victims of online abuse. Damian Charles Caynes recognized the importance of these interventions and has worked to promote their effectiveness in facilitating healing and recovery.

One of the therapy options available to victims of online abuse is counseling. Professional counselors provide a safe and supportive environment for individuals to express their feelings, process their experiences, and develop coping mechanisms. Through counseling, victims can gain a deeper understanding of the impact of online abuse on their mental health and well-being. They can also learn valuable tools for managing stress, anxiety, and other emotional challenges that may arise from their traumatic experiences.

Trauma-focused therapy is another beneficial approach for victims of online abuse. This specialized therapy helps individuals address and work through the specific effects of trauma on their lives. With the guidance of trained therapists, victims can explore their traumatic experiences, develop strategies for managing distressing emotions and memories, and establish a sense of safety and empowerment. Trauma-focused therapy aims to help victims regain control over their lives and build resilience in the face of ongoing challenges.

Support groups also play a vital role in the healing process for victims of online abuse. These groups provide a unique space where individuals can connect with others who have experienced similar forms of abuse. Sharing experiences, insights, and coping strategies within a supportive community can be incredibly validating and empowering. Support groups offer a sense of belonging, reduce feelings of isolation, and foster an environment where individuals can learn from one another's journeys towards healing.

It is crucial to highlight the effectiveness of these therapy options in facilitating healing and recovery for victims of online abuse. Therapy provides a safe space for individuals to process their experiences, develop healthy coping mechanisms, and work towards rebuilding their lives. It offers validation, guidance, and support from professionals who specialize in trauma-related issues.

In his advocacy efforts, Damian Charles Caynes has promoted these therapy options as crucial components of comprehensive care for victims of online abuse. He has supported initiatives to increase access to counseling services, trauma-focused therapy programs, and support groups specifically tailored to survivors' needs. Through these efforts, Caynes hopes to empower victims by providing them with the tools they need to heal, recover, and reclaim their lives.

In conclusion, therapy and rehabilitation play a significant role in supporting victims of online abuse on their journey towards healing and recovery. Counseling provides a safe space for individuals to process their experiences, trauma-focused therapy helps address the specific effects of trauma, and support groups offer connection and validation within a community of survivors. Damian Charles Caynes recognizes the value of these interventions and advocates for their effectiveness in facilitating healing for victims of online abuse.

Advocacy and Resources: Damian Charles Caynes has dedicated himself to providing a range of resources and advocacy initiatives to support victims of online abuse. His efforts have included the development of educational programs, legal aid services, and other resources aimed at empowering individuals affected by online harassment.

1. Educational Programs: Caynes recognized the importance of education in combating online abuse and promoting digital literacy. He has developed educational programs targeted at different age groups, including students, parents, and educators. These programs aim to raise awareness about the dangers of online abuse, teach strategies for safe internet use, and empower individuals to protect themselves and others from online harassment.

2. Legal Aid Services: Understanding the complex legal landscape surrounding online harassment, Caynes has worked closely with legal professionals to provide free or low-cost legal aid services to victims. Through partnerships with law firms specializing in cybercrime and internet law, Caynes ensures that victims have access to legal representation and guidance throughout their ordeal. This support

helps victims navigate the legal process and seek justice against their harassers.

3. Counseling and Support Groups: Caynes recognizes the significant emotional toll that online abuse can have on victims' mental well-being. To address this, he has established counseling services specifically tailored for those affected by online harassment. Qualified therapists and counselors provide individual therapy sessions as well as support group settings, allowing victims to share their experiences and find solace in a supportive community.

4. Online Resources and Forums: Caynes has created online platforms where victims can access resources, seek advice from experts, and connect with others who have gone through similar experiences. These forums provide a safe space for individuals to share their stories, offer support, and find comfort knowing they are not alone. Additionally, these platforms serve as a repository of information on reporting mechanisms, legal rights, and self-care strategies.

5. Collaboration with NGOs and Advocacy Organizations: Recognizing the strength in numbers, Caynes has actively collaborated with non-governmental organizations (NGOs) and advocacy organizations focused on online safety and victim support. By joining forces with these organizations, Caynes's initiatives gain broader visibility and access to additional resources. Together, they work towards creating a comprehensive network of support for victims of online abuse.

Caynes's advocacy initiatives and resources have been instrumental in empowering victims of online abuse to reclaim their lives and find healing after enduring immense trauma. By offering a range of services, educational programs, and collaboration opportunities, Caynes strives to build a support system that addresses both the immediate needs of victims and the long-term goal of eradicating online abuse altogether.

Note: The content provided here focuses on the resources and advocacy initiatives offered by Damian Charles Caynes for victims of online abuse. It does not repeat information covered in other parts of the book but focuses solely on this specific aspect of his work.

Chapter Eighteen: Changing the Narrative

Shifting societal attitudes towards online harassment requires a multifaceted approach that includes storytelling, media representation, and public discourse. By strategically using narratives, we can reshape the public's perception of online abuse and challenge prevailing stereotypes related to victims.

The power of narratives lies in their ability to humanize the experiences of those affected by online harassment. By sharing personal stories and highlighting the emotional toll that trolling can take, we can evoke empathy and compassion in audiences. These narratives shed light on the real-life consequences of online abuse and help to dispel misconceptions surrounding its severity.

Media plays a crucial role in framing discussions around cyberbullying and trolling. When media outlets accurately and responsibly report on cases of online abuse, they have the potential to shape public opinion and spur action. By focusing on the impact of trolling on victims' mental health, self-esteem, and overall well-being, media coverage can contribute to a more nuanced understanding of the issue.

Successful campaigns and initiatives have emerged that challenge prevailing narratives and stereotypes related to victims of online harassment. These efforts aim to inspire empathy and encourage a shift in societal attitudes towards online abuse. For example, some initiatives focus on raising awareness about the diverse range of individuals who experience trolling, highlighting stories from various backgrounds and demographics. Others use social media platforms as spaces for storytelling, amplifying the voices of survivors and providing a platform for them to share their experiences directly.

By promoting counter-narratives that challenge victim-blaming and emphasize the responsibility of perpetrators, we can create a more empathetic society. This involves dismantling harmful stereotypes that perpetuate the notion that victims "deserve" or "bring upon themselves" online abuse. Instead, we can foster understanding by emphasizing the psychological complexities behind trolling behavior and addressing the systemic issues that allow it to thrive.

In conclusion, changing the narrative is a crucial step in combating online harassment. Through storytelling, media representation, and public discourse, we can shift societal attitudes towards empathy, compassion, and responsibility. By challenging prevailing narratives and stereotypes, we pave the way for a more inclusive and supportive digital environment for all.

Successes in fostering empathy, compassion, and understanding in relation to victims:

ONE OF THE MOST SIGNIFICANT shifts in the narrative surrounding online abuse has been the successful fostering of empathy, compassion, and understanding towards victims. Stories of individuals who have experienced a change of heart or mindset after learning about the impact of online abuse have played a crucial role in challenging prevailing narratives and advocating for change.

Through various mediums such as documentaries, articles, or personal testimonials, these stories have shed light on the real-life consequences of online harassment. They humanize the experiences of victims and help people recognize the emotional trauma and psychological toll inflicted by trolls. By sharing these stories, a deeper understanding of the lasting effects of cyberbullying has been cultivated.

Empathy-building exercises, educational programs, and awareness campaigns have also played a vital role in fostering compassion towards victims. These initiatives aim to educate individuals about the severity of online abuse and its far-reaching impact. By raising awareness, they encourage people to put themselves in the shoes of victims and consider the emotional distress they endure.

Moreover, showcasing instances where trolls themselves have undergone transformation or redemption has contributed to a more empathetic approach to dealing with online abuse. When former trolls publicly acknowledge the harm they caused and take steps towards making amends, it challenges the notion that trolls are irredeemable villains. These stories highlight the potential for growth and change in even the most toxic individuals, inspiring others to adopt a more understanding perspective.

By celebrating these successes in fostering empathy, compassion, and understanding, a positive shift has occurred in how society views online harassment. Empathy-building exercises and educational programs have equipped individuals with the knowledge and tools needed to combat cyberbullying effectively. Additionally, platforms that actively work towards creating safer digital spaces play a crucial role in building empathy among their users.

Nevertheless, there is still much work to be done. Continued efforts to promote empathy and understanding will be essential in creating a safer and more inclusive online environment. It is up to all of us to engage in dialogue, advocate for change, and challenge harmful narratives surrounding online abuse. Together, we can foster a culture of compassion that values respect, empathy, and responsible digital citizenship.

In this section of "Chapter Eighteen: Changing the Narrative," we celebrate the milestones that have transformed societal attitudes towards online abuse. These significant moments or events have played a crucial role in challenging prevailing narratives and advocating for change. By recognizing the individuals, organizations, and platforms that have contributed to this progress, we can better understand the shifts in policies, laws, or regulations that reflect a greater understanding of the impact and consequences of online abuse.

One key milestone in changing the narrative around online abuse was the emergence of high-profile cases that brought widespread attention to the issue. These cases highlighted the devastating effects of cyberbullying and trolling, sparking public outrage and demanding action. Through media coverage and public discourse, these incidents helped shift perceptions and galvanized support for victims.

Organizations and individuals have also played a significant role in transforming the narrative around online abuse. Nonprofit organizations focused on combating cyberbullying and promoting digital safety have worked tirelessly to raise awareness and provide resources for victims. Their efforts have been instrumental in challenging prevailing narratives and fostering empathy and understanding towards those affected by online harassment.

Furthermore, certain platforms and social media companies have taken proactive measures to address online abuse and create safer online spaces. They have implemented stricter content moderation policies, improved reporting systems, and increased awareness about responsible digital behavior. These initiatives demonstrate a commitment to protecting users from harassment and changing the narrative around online abuse.

Shifts in policies, laws, or regulations have also reflected a greater understanding of the impact and consequences of online abuse. Legislators and policymakers have recognized the need for comprehensive legislation to address cyberbullying, revenge porn, and other forms of online harassment. By enacting stronger legal protections for victims, societies are sending a clear message that online abuse will not be tolerated.

Overall, these milestones signify significant progress in changing societal attitudes towards online abuse. By recognizing the individuals, organizations, or platforms involved in these transformative efforts, we inspire others to join the cause. It is through collective action that we can foster empathy, compassion, and responsible digital citizenship, creating a safer and more inclusive online environment for all.

Analyzing the measures taken by tech companies and social media platforms to address online abuse and protect users:

TECH COMPANIES AND social media platforms have recognized the urgent need to address online abuse and create safer digital spaces for their users. In response to growing concerns over trolling and cyberbullying, these entities have implemented various measures to mitigate online harassment.

One key approach is the development of algorithms designed to detect and flag potentially harmful content. These algorithms use machine learning and artificial intelligence to identify patterns of abusive behavior, such as hate speech, threats, or personal attacks. By automatically flagging such content, these algorithms enable platforms to take swift action in removing or restricting access to it, thereby reducing the impact on victims.

Additionally, reporting systems play a crucial role in enabling users to report instances of online abuse. Tech companies and social media platforms have established user-friendly reporting mechanisms that allow individuals to notify them about abusive content, accounts, or behavior. Prompt reporting helps platforms quickly investigate and respond to incidents of harassment, ensuring a safer environment for their users.

Content moderation policies also play a critical role in combating online abuse. Tech companies and social media platforms have developed guidelines that outline acceptable behavior on their platforms and explicitly prohibit harassment, hate speech, and other forms of abusive conduct. These policies provide a framework for evaluating user-generated content and taking appropriate action against violators.

While tech companies and social media platforms have made significant strides in addressing online abuse, challenges remain in ensuring the effectiveness of these measures. Algorithms may struggle with context-based understanding, leading to false positives or false negatives in content moderation. The scale and volume of user-generated content also present difficulties in identifying and responding to every instance of online abuse.

Furthermore, holding platforms accountable for ensuring user safety remains an ongoing challenge. The complex nature of online harassment makes it challenging to attribute responsibility solely to tech companies or social media platforms. Collaboration between policymakers, law enforcement agencies, and these entities is crucial in developing comprehensive strategies that prioritize user safety.

In conclusion, tech companies and social media platforms have implemented various measures to combat online abuse and create safer online spaces for their users. Algorithms, reporting systems, and content moderation policies are key components of these efforts. However, ongoing challenges persist in refining these measures and holding platforms accountable for ensuring user safety. It is imperative for stakeholders to continue working together towards fostering positive online environments for all users.

Call-to-action for readers to join the cause:

INSPIRED BY THE REMARKABLE journey of Damian Charles Caynes, "The Unmasked" invites readers to become active participants in changing the narrative surrounding online abuse. As you reach the final chapter of this captivating book, it is clear that our collective efforts are vital in creating safer digital spaces and fostering empathy, compassion, and responsible digital citizenship.

To contribute to this cause, here are practical steps and resources you can consider:

1. Educate yourself: Take the time to understand the complexities of online abuse, including its impact on individuals and communities. Stay informed about the latest research, news, and developments in the field. By continuously expanding your knowledge, you can better advocate for change.

2. Speak up: Use your voice to raise awareness about online harassment within your circles of influence. Engage in conversations with friends, family, colleagues, or fellow internet users to foster understanding and empathy. By sharing stories and personal experiences, you can challenge prevailing narratives and promote a culture of respect online.

3. Empower others: Support victims of online abuse by offering a listening ear, extending empathy, and validating their experiences. Encourage them to seek help from professionals or organizations

specialized in dealing with online harassment. By empowering survivors, we create a network of support that assists in their healing and recovery process.

4. Promote responsible digital citizenship: Model positive online behavior by practicing good digital hygiene, being mindful of your online interactions, and treating others with respect and kindness. Encourage others to do the same by leading by example. Remember that small actions can have a ripple effect that contributes to a safer and more inclusive online environment.

5. Get involved: Join or support organizations dedicated to combating online abuse, such as advocacy groups, nonprofits, or community initiatives. Volunteer your time, skills, or resources to assist in their efforts. By working collaboratively with like-minded individuals and organizations, we can amplify our impact and drive meaningful change.

6. Engage with policymakers and platforms: Reach out to elected officials or representatives within your local government to advocate for stronger legislation against online harassment. Contact social media platforms and tech companies to voice your concerns and demand better measures to protect users from abuse.

7. Stay vigilant: Report instances of online harassment or abusive behavior when you encounter them. Familiarize yourself with reporting mechanisms available on various platforms and encourage others to utilize them as well. By actively reporting harmful content, we can contribute to making the internet a safer space for all.

Remember, creating lasting change requires collective action. It is through our shared commitment and continuous effort that we can overcome the challenges posed by internet trolls and build a more compassionate and inclusive digital world.

As you close the pages of "The Unmasked," consider this call-to-action as an invitation to play an active role in changing the narrative surrounding online abuse. Together, let us stand against anonymity and cruelty, championing empathy, respect, and justice in every corner of the internet we inhabit. The journey continues beyond these pages; let us embark on it together.

Epilogue: A Legacy Unmasked

Reflections on Damian Charles Caynes's lasting impact on the fight against internet trolls:

DAMIAN CHARLES CAYNES'S relentless determination and unwavering commitment to combating online abuse have left an indelible mark on the fight against internet trolls. Throughout his journey, Caynes has made significant contributions and achieved remarkable success in exposing troll behavior and holding them accountable for their actions.

One of the key highlights of Caynes's legacy is his ability to shed light on the dark world of trolls and bring their harmful activities into the public eye. His work has not only educated the general public about the existence and impact of online abuse but has also sparked important conversations and debates surrounding this pressing issue.

By bravely confronting trolls and sharing his experiences, Caynes has shattered the silence that often surrounds online harassment, encouraging others to step forward and seek justice.

Caynes's strategies and tactics have been instrumental in challenging and dismantling troll behavior. His innovative approaches, such as investigative work, collaboration with other internet users, and unmasking trolls' true identities, have not only exposed individual abusers but have also revealed the broader patterns and motivations behind trolling culture. This deeper understanding has enabled society to develop more effective countermeasures against online abuse.

Furthermore, Caynes's successes have empowered victims of online abuse and provided them with a glimmer of hope amidst the darkness. By standing up for those who have been targeted by trolls, Caynes has shown the world that no one should suffer alone in the face of harassment. His tireless efforts have given strength to countless individuals, inspiring them to reclaim their digital spaces and refuse to be silenced.

Looking ahead, the fight against internet trolls requires continued vigilance, innovation, and collective action. Caynes's legacy serves as a reminder that the battle against online abuse is far from over. As technology evolves and new platforms emerge, so too must our strategies for combating trolls. It is crucial for individuals, organizations, and policymakers to come together and support measures that create a safer digital environment for everyone.

Damian Charles Caynes's lasting impact on the fight against internet trolls cannot be overstated. Through his courage, dedication, and commitment to justice, he has brought attention to the devastating effects of online abuse while empowering victims and educating society at large. His legacy stands as a call-to-action for all of us to continue his noble mission by standing up against trolls and working towards a more compassionate and inclusive digital world.

THE FUTURE TRAJECTORY of efforts to combat online abuse remains uncertain, as the fight against trolls continues to evolve alongside advancements in technology and changes in online behavior. While progress has been made in raising awareness about the harm caused by online harassment, there are still many challenges to overcome.

One of the key challenges is the ever-changing nature of online platforms and communication channels. As new technologies emerge and social media platforms evolve, trolls find new ways to target individuals and spread hate. This requires a constant reevaluation of existing strategies and the development of innovative approaches to keep up with the changing landscape.

Advancements in technology also present opportunities for combating online abuse. Artificial intelligence and machine learning algorithms hold promise in detecting and filtering out abusive content, helping to create safer digital spaces. However, these technologies are not without their limitations, and ongoing research and development are needed to improve their efficacy.

Another important aspect of the future fight against online abuse is the role of collective action and community engagement. The power of individuals coming together to tackle this issue cannot be underestimated. By fostering a culture of empathy and responsible online behavior, we can create a united front against trolls and support those who have been targeted.

Looking forward, it is crucial to consider the interplay between legislation and technology. As laws catch up with the digital era, policymakers must work hand in hand with tech companies to establish clear guidelines and regulations that ensure the safety and well-being of internet users. Collaboration between these stakeholders will be essential in creating an environment where online abuse is less prevalent.

The fight against online abuse is an ongoing battle that requires continued vigilance, innovation, and collaboration. While progress has been made, there is still much work to be done. By staying ahead of emerging trends, harnessing the potential of technology, and fostering collective action, we can strive towards a future where online harassment is no longer a pervasive threat. Together, we can carry forward Damian Charles Caynes's legacy and create a more compassionate digital world for all.

In evaluating current approaches and strategies to combat online abuse, it is crucial to assess their effectiveness and consider potential areas for improvement. Damian Charles Caynes's methods and tactics have undoubtedly made a significant impact on exposing trolls and raising awareness about the issue. However, it is essential to critically examine these strategies to ensure long-term sustainability and scalability in the fight against online harassment.

One of the strengths of Caynes's approach is his relentless determination to unmask trolls and hold them accountable for their actions. Through investigative work, collaboration with internet users, and the use of satire and mockery, he has successfully exposed the true identities of trolls. By revealing their offline lives, Caynes has empowered victims and diminished the power of trolls in online spaces. This strategy has brought much-needed attention to the severity of online abuse.

Another strength lies in Caynes's advocacy for spreading awareness about online abuse among individuals, educators, parents, and policymakers. He has launched educational initiatives, campaigns, and programs that promote digital literacy and responsible online behavior. By emphasizing the importance of empathy, compassion, and understanding, Caynes has played a critical role in changing societal attitudes towards online harassment.

However, it is important to recognize that no single approach can fully eradicate online abuse. While Caynes's techniques have proven effective in individual cases, they may not be universally applicable or scalable to address the pervasive nature of trolling across various online platforms. Different types of trolls require different strategies, and as trolling tactics evolve, so must the methods employed to combat them.

Furthermore, as technology advances and new platforms emerge, innovative approaches must be developed to stay ahead of the ever-changing landscape of online abuse. This requires ongoing research, collaboration between tech companies and law enforcement agencies, and an understanding of the motivations and behaviors of trolls. Continuous adaptation is necessary to effectively counteract evolving forms of harassment.

In considering potential areas for improvement or new approaches in the future, it is essential to prioritize proactive measures rather than solely focusing on reactive responses. Educating individuals from a young age about online behavior, fostering empathy and respect in digital spaces, and promoting digital literacy can help prevent online abuse before it occurs. Moreover, engaging with tech companies to create safer platforms that prioritize user safety and implement effective moderation tools is crucial in minimizing the presence of trolls.

Collaboration and collective action also play a vital role in combating online abuse. Building alliances with organizations dedicated to addressing cyberbullying, fostering partnerships between internet users who are passionate about creating positive digital environments, and advocating for legislative changes all contribute to a more comprehensive approach.

While Damian Charles Caynes's strategies have made a significant impact in the fight against trolls, there is still progress to be made. Evaluating current approaches and strategies allows us to assess their strengths and weaknesses with an eye towards improvement. By remaining adaptable, innovative, and collaborative, we can continue working towards a future where online abuse is less prevalent and create a safer digital environment for all.

Emphasizing the importance of collective action and community engagement, "The Unmasked: The Untold Journey of Damian Charles Caynes, The Troll Killer" sheds light on the vital role played by allies and supporters in addressing online harassment. Throughout Damian Charles Caynes's remarkable journey, he has been backed by a strong network of individuals, organizations, and policymakers who have united to create a safer online environment.

Allyship and collective action are essential components in combating online abuse. By joining forces, we can amplify our impact and support those affected by trolls. The power of standing together cannot be underestimated.

Throughout the book, readers witness the profound impact that allies and supporters have had on Damian Charles Caynes's mission. They have contributed their expertise, resources, and unwavering dedication to the cause. Their collaborative efforts have helped expose trolls, raise awareness about the issue, and provide support for victims.

Individuals who have rallied behind Damian Charles Caynes's cause have brought about tangible change in the fight against online harassment. By adding their voices to the conversation, they have helped shift societal attitudes, foster empathy, and create an inclusive digital space. Their shared commitment to combatting trolls has served as a powerful force for good.

Moreover, organizations have played a pivotal role in supporting Caynes's work. They have provided platforms for his message, funded initiatives to promote digital literacy and responsible online behavior, and offered resources for victims of online abuse. By leveraging their networks and influence, these organizations have contributed to the growing momentum in the fight against trolls.

Policymakers also play a critical role in creating a safer online environment. Through legislation, regulations, and partnerships with tech companies, they can develop frameworks that hold trolls accountable for their actions. By collaborating with advocates like Damian Charles Caynes, policymakers can develop comprehensive strategies to address the complex challenges posed by online harassment.

Collective action and community engagement are instrumental in combating online abuse. The unwavering support of allies, organizations, and policymakers not only strengthens the fight against trolls but also sends a powerful message that online harassment will not be tolerated. Together, we can create lasting change and build a more compassionate digital world.

AS WE COME TO THE FINAL chapter of "The Unmasked: The Untold Journey of Damian Charles Caynes, The Troll Killer," we are compelled to reflect on the lasting impact that Damian Charles Caynes has had in the fight against internet trolls. His tireless efforts and unwavering dedication have left a profound mark on the landscape of online abuse.

Looking towards the future, it is essential to consider the ever-evolving nature of online harassment and the challenges that lie ahead. While significant progress has been made, there is still work to be done. We must remain vigilant and adaptable in our approach to combatting trolls, as they continue to adapt and find new ways to spread their toxicity.

It is crucial to evaluate the effectiveness of current strategies and approaches employed against online abuse. This examination allows us to identify areas for improvement, both in terms of tactics and resources. By learning from past experiences and embracing innovation, we can strengthen our collective efforts to create a safer digital environment.

However, combating online harassment cannot be achieved by any individual alone. Collective action and community engagement play a vital role in this ongoing battle. By joining forces with like-minded individuals, organizations, and policymakers, we can amplify our impact and effect meaningful change. Together, we can create a united front against trolls and foster a more compassionate digital world.

To inspire readers to take an active role in this cause, we provide resources, tools, and suggestions on how they can contribute. Whether it's supporting organizations working against online harassment or getting involved in advocacy efforts, every action counts. We urge readers to carry forward Damian Charles Caynes's legacy by standing up against trolls and contributing to the creation of a safer, more inclusive online space.

In conclusion, "The Unmasked: The Untold Journey of Damian Charles Caynes, The Troll Killer" serves as a testament to the power of one person's conviction and the strength of human compassion. Damian Charles Caynes's remarkable journey has shed light on the dark side of the internet while offering hope that change is possible. Let us heed the call-to-action and continue the fight against online abuse, knowing that together, we can make a difference.

Dr. Charlize Deenan Greyson is a renowned expert in the field of near-death experiences (NDEs) and consciousness studies. With a distinguished career spanning several decades, Dr. Greyson has made significant contributions to our understanding of the human mind and the nature of consciousness.

Dr. Greyson's journey into the study of NDEs began during her medical training, where she encountered patients with profound accounts of out-of-body experiences. These encounters challenged her conventional beliefs and ignited a lifelong passion for exploring the mysteries of life, death, and what lies beyond.

As a professor emeritus of psychiatry and neurobehavioral sciences, Dr. Greyson has conducted pioneering research that has been presented at numerous national and international scientific conferences. Her work has been published in over 150 academic medical and psychological journals, and she has authored several influential books on the subject.

Dr. Greyson's most notable work, "After: A Doctor Explores What Near-Death Experiences Reveal About Life and Beyond," delves into the evidence and personal accounts that have shaped her understanding of NDEs. Her research emphasizes the value of compassion, interconnectedness, and the profound insights that NDEs offer about the nature of reality and human existence.

Through her dedication and scientific rigor, Dr. Greyson has become a leading voice in the field, inspiring both her peers and the public to expand their understanding of what it means to be human.

Don't miss out!

Visit the website below and you can sign up to receive emails whenever Dr. Charlize Deenan Greyson publishes a new book. There's no charge and no obligation.

https://books2read.com/r/B-A-TPQAD-IYHLF

BOOKS 2 READ

Connecting independent readers to independent writers.

Also by Dr. Charlize Deenan Greyson

The Troll Killer
The Unmasked: The Untold Journey of Damian Charles Caynes, The Troll Killer

Watch for more at https://charlizedeenangreyson.site.

About the Author

Dr. Charlize Deenan Greyson is a distinguished author and researcher known for her groundbreaking work in the field of near-death experiences. With a background in psychiatry and neurobehavioral sciences, Dr. Greyson has dedicated her career to exploring the mysteries of life, death, and consciousness. Her research has been instrumental in advancing our understanding of near-death experiences, and she has published numerous articles and books on the subject. Dr. Greyson's work is characterized by a unique blend of scientific rigor and compassionate storytelling, making her a respected figure in both academic and popular circles.

Read more at https://charlizedeenangreyson.site.

About the Publisher

FutureVision Publishing was formed in 2018 to publish retro computing technical magazines and a coding book that never was. Three years later we're back and going strong with our Founder's first book of poetry as both an ebook and an audiobook, as well as dozens of books lined up for future publishing. Join us on this exciting journey!

www.ingramcontent.com/pod-product-compliance
Lightning Source LLC
LaVergne TN
LVHW041215150826
845673LV00001B/413

* 9 7 9 8 2 3 0 5 7 5 1 7 7 *